SUNSHINE STYLE

A SUNNY CARIBBEE COOKBOOK

for Sunny Climes and Limin' Times

Susan Gunter

Published by Sunny Caribbee Spice Co.
PO Box 3237 VDA
Charlotte Amalie
St. Thomas
Virgin Islands 00803-3237
809-494-2178 Phone
809-494-4039 Fax

Library of Congress Cataloging-in-Publication Data
Library of Congress Catalog Card Number: 94-092045
Main entry under title:
Sunshine Style.
    1. Cookbook
I. Gunter, Susan
First Edition

ISBN 0-9639423-0-1

Designed by Susan Gunter and Joan Walsh
Cover Art and Interior Graphics by M.L. Etre
Printed by Henry N. Sawyer Company, Inc.

For my Mother, Father and Brother;
Mary, Andy and Peter Anderson

Acknowledgements

During the several years that I have struggled to write **Sunshine Style**, numerous people encouraged my progress along the rocky road to my elusive destination. My heartfelt thanks to the following:

Lisa Gunter Fresne, my daughter and special friend … always cheerful and helpful … for the many roles she has played in the **Sunshine Style** scenario: editor, advisor, recipe contributor and morale booster … and **David**, her husband, also full of ideas and enthusiasm.

Joan Walsh (latterly assisted by **Wendy Kury**), who has taken my scrawled messages and coffee stained notes and miraculously composed them all into a beautiful, readable book. I couldn't have done it without her.

Greg Gunter who is always "there" smiling and supportive.

Jeanne Bach-Clark, charter boat chef extraordinaire, whose cruising cuisine exemplifies **Sunshine Style** … for her continuing support and her innovative recipes and hints.

Althea and **Chan** who translated much of my first works onto paper, **Rosetta**, with us from the beginning, **Caroline** and all the loyal **Sunny Caribbee staff** who have contributed a wealth of local lore.

Lisa Etre, celebrated Caribbean artist, for her ever brilliant artwork.

Jonathan Sawyer our printer and friend, who successfully puts everything together.

Carol and Mark Gunter and all my family and friends who have influenced my life foodwise and other wise, for being patient with my impatience to write this book, and who have survived my trial and error recipe testings…

And most of all —

Bob, my husband, best friend and faithful fan who has cooked, cleaned, shopped, run errands and dealt with all manner of things… prevailing through all, enabling me to accomplish my goal.

In the beginning …
Sunny Caribbee Spice Co.

Our story began over three decades ago when we first fled southward for a Caribbean holiday. The diverse island cultures (love of the food, music, art and crafts, the natural beauty) kept enticing us to restyle our lives. In 1979, carefully weighing the merits of various islands from Jamaica to Grenada, and after much soul-searching and a certain amount of trepidation, we chose Tortola to be our Island Home.

In 1980 upon completion of our "Magic House" we plotted the next phase of "The Paradise Plan." Determined not to sit on the beach drinking rum every day, we stockpiled our thoughts to resolve what would fulfill our expectations and ideals of life on a Tropical Isle. What would sustain our lives and energies as we embarked on our Caribbean adventure?

An idea was born ! We began to create a unique and distinctive venture reflecting the true spirit of the Caribbean. Our concept to cultivate, foster and renew the production of indigenous food and craft products while providing jobs and restoring pride in local talent was encouraged and approved by the British Virgin Islands Government in 1982. Thus began a decade of adventure that would take us to every corner of the Antilles (thru several hurricanes, a few revolutions and once almost into a Haitian Jail).

The year of creation was a whirlwind of activity … mixing, blending, printing, designing, traveling, meeting and working with hundreds of people … learning and listening. Our "Magic House" became the experimental station for numerous island-inspired concoctions and a production center for **Spicee Catsup, Rum Peppers** and **Pure Vanilla**. We burnt our tongues tasting and perpetually exuded an aroma of exotic, tropical fragrances. Patience was not only a virtue but a necessity.

After an exhausting but fascinating year of preparation we opened the doors to **SUNNY CARIBBEE** in November 1983 … in Raffie Stout's Building by the roundabout, with a staff of 3-1/2 (Bob, Susan, Greg and the part-time help of our housekeeper). The challenging first year of operation was a trial in living as well as working. In our mini-quarters, everything happened: mixing, packing, storing, buying, selling, bookkeeping. A little success inspired us to continually add to our array of products and staff.

Bursting our seams at Raffies and giving up the battle of the goats, our search for a new location concluded with a move in 1986 to H.R. Penn's "Social Inn," (first guest house in Tortola) … a quaint, West Indian building. We have been happily ensconced in our miniature "Spice factory," on Old main Street, ever since. Here we share with our love of all things Caribbean.

Miraculously, during the past ten years we have also opened The Caribbean Marketplace in St. Thomas, a boutique and art gallery at Skyworld in Tortola, two licensed **SUNNY CARIBBEE** Shops, and a full-fledged art gallery in Roadtown. We continue to wholesale to boutiques throughout the Caribbean and to spice up the lives of people all over the world by mail order.

As we catch our breath and reflect on all the wondrous things that have occurred in our "second lives," we feel very fortunate to have achieved our goals. We have our space in Paradise and have helped to restore and present an image and product of a proud, talented, complex people in this extraordinary part of the world.

Sushine Style Scenario

Now that **Sunny Caribbee Spice Co.** is an integral part of my life, the secret ambition to write a cookbook has naturally evolved in the "Paradise Plan". This desire has been encouraged by family, friends and customers who often remark "looks, smells, sounds great ... but what do you do with it?"

Sunshine Style will acquaint you with the many flavours of **Sunny Caribbee Spice Co.** all influenced by places in the sun. There are 28 menus and 175 simple, but delicious, carefree and creative recipes to help you achieve your own "Sunshine Style." The body of the book is organized into 8 chapters based upon different times of day, progressing from dawn to dark with accompanying venues, menus, trivia and tips. The menus are designed to suit the occasion and locale with recipes that complement each other both in taste and presentation. **Dash, Splash and Sprinkle** lists imaginative uses for **Sunny Caribbee** products while **Paradise Pantry** describes the products and their ingredients. An additional treat is **Guest Quarters**, a collection of recipes contributed by customers, family and friends.

Sunshine Style recipes are based upon good, flavourful and fresh provisions readily available almost everywhere. They concentrate on natural herbs, spices, seasonings, sauces and preserves to enhance rather than mask the flavours of "real food". Consequently, the need for extra flavour often obtained from excess fat, salt, sugar or chemical additives is eliminated. There are very few recipes that contain "packaged" or junk foods and whenever possible, fresh meat, fish, and produce are preferable. Low fat everything and very few calorie-laden desserts are found in my book. The rich variety of wholesome, uncomplicated recipes will reward the most discriminating master or novice chef. Eating healthfully and simply is to eat deliciously well.

You will discover many recipes to be excitingly innovative while others you will enjoy as variations of old favourites. Wherever you may be ... on a lake in the Midwest ... a yacht in the "Med" ... a tropical isle ... atop a mountain in Vermont ... or in your own back yard ... this book is written for you in the spirit of Sunshine and endless Summer.

Table of Contents

VENUES, MENUS & RECIPES

I. Bright Beginnings

II. Sunshine Snack Attack

III. Brilliant Brunches

IV. Luscious Lunches

V. Tea Time Teasers

VI. Sundowners

VII. Divine Dinners

VIII. Celestial Snacks & Sumptuous Suppers

Guest Quarters

Paradise Pantry

Dash Splash & Sprinkle

Index

Miscellaneous

Sunshine Style

Sunshine Style is a celebration of good times and the art of good living. It is being with family and friends in happy places, enjoying the spiritual warmth of the sun, and making every day festive and fun. It is also having time to relax and enjoy good food, conversation and laughter without being a slave to galley, kitchen or convention.

Living my life in the sun has probably been an unwitting dream since I was a child growing up by the sea. The pleasure of my many activities has always been enhanced by being out of doors where there is a certain spirit of peace and freedom. This preference for fresh, clean air, the smell of the sea, flowers and trees, the sunlit colours influenced and determined what I think, how I work and play, and who I am.

Cooking for family and friends, inventing and experimenting with food and flavours was childhood play and after marriage and the arrival of children became a full time vocation. I enjoyed the challenge of presenting good food attractively, even when the odds of doing so with a young family were overwhelming. My efforts weren't always successful, but meals at our home were never dull and usually commanded attention and a certain amount of respect.

Most credit for my culinary achievement must go to my mother, an intuitive "avant garde" cook, whose influence has been passed along also to my husband and three children who all display creative clout in the kitchen. While many Americans in the "thirties" and "forties" were eating bland, overcooked, uninspired food, my mother's zesty and innovative meals were an everyday occurance. Her use of Herbs, Seasonings, and Sauces along with flair and imagination made her a unique "no recipe cook," with "real food" always the essential main ingredient. Living by the sea provided us a constant supply of fresh seafood: Mussels, Moonshells, Haddock, Sole, and Lobster. My father's "Victory Garden" rewarded us with an endless array of vegetables and a brilliant selection of home preserved goodies that would tide us over until the next summer's fresh bounty. **Tomato Special, Grape Conserve, Mulberry Jam, Kentucky Wonders** and pickled everything marched in a colourful parade along the shelves. Little did we know that we were on the cutting edge of Culinary Chic.

Now decades later, our pantry shelves still reflect my mother's style blended with the influence of our many years of holiday and business travel. We always seem to gravitate to "Sunshine Places" (the Caribbean, the Mediterranean Countries, the Greek Isles and the warmest of the United States) where heritage is vividly portrayed in "Cuisines of the Sun." Spanning many cultures and ethnic traditions, these cuisines are similar and compatible in their utilization of local and indigenous produce, herbs, spices, meat and fish to create robust and distinctive cooking styles.

The highlight of our travels is our ritual visit to the outdoor market. This microcosm of regional colour, aroma, activity and spectacle is where we discover and delight in the real substance of a country's people and their culture. The markets, the specialty stores, the farms and the vineyards are all adventures forever instilled in my mind.

Surely my move to the Caribbean was a predestined journey and the creation of **Sunny Caribbee** by Bob, Greg and me has been the culmination of that journey and of my dreams and my quest to live in **Sunshine Style**.

I

Bright Beginnings

It's going to be a giant day.

Let's pack a few goodies,

fill a thermos or two,

go to the beach and watch

the sun rise.

Bananarama

Curried Eggs Diablo

Cheddar Chutney Bacon Biscuits

Trinidad Coffee

Serves 2-4

Bananarama

2 ripe bananas
1-1/2 c. ice water
1/2 c. low fat yogurt
2 Tbs. **West Indian Honey** ☀
1 tsp. **Guavaberry Liqueur** ☀

- Combine all ingredients in blender.*
- Blend until smooth and well mixed.
- Pour into glass (or thermos).
- Grate nutmeg over top.

makes approx. two 12 oz. servings

* Add 4-5 fresh strawberries, 3/4 to 1 c. mango or papaya for a different flavour treat

Curried Eggs Diablo

3 large hard boiled eggs*
2 Tbs. minced scallions
2-1/2 Tbs. mayonnaise (lite)
1-1/2 tsp. **Caribbee Curry** ☀

- Shell eggs and cut into halves.
- Remove yolks and mash.
- Add remaining ingredients and mix well.**
- Lightly refill white half with curry mixture.
- Sprinkle with minced parsley or chives.

* Perfectly Boiled Eggs

Place eggs in a saucepan with enough cold water to cover by an inch. Add 2 Tbs. vinegar to prevent cracking. Cover pan and bring to a rolling boil. Simmer for 5 min. Remove from heat and let sit covered for 15-18 min. (depending on size of egg). Drain and run cold water over eggs to stop cooking. Tap shell gently, rolling between hands and peel under cold water.

**Bits of leftover ham or bacon are a good addition to yolk mixture, especially for lunch or appetizers.

Cheddar Chutney Bacon Biscuits

1 c. all purpose flour
1-1/2 tsp. baking powder
1/2 tsp. **Seasoned Sea Salt** ☀
2 Tbs. softened unsalted butter
1/2 c. coarsely grated sharp
  cheddar cheese
2–3 Tbs. **Mango Chutney** ☀
  (finely chopped)
1/3 c. milk
1/2 c. cooked bacon bits (or cooked
  sausage or ham bits)

- Preheat oven to 450°
- In bowl mix flour, baking powder
  and **Seasoned Sea Salt** ☀
- Add butter and blend (mix will be
  crumbly)
- Stir in cheddar cheese
- Combine milk and **Mango
  Chutney** ☀ and add to mixture
- Add bacon and mix lightly
- Drop dough into 6 mounds in well
  buttered 9 in. round baking dish
- Bake about 15 minutes or until
  golden brown

〰 Fill your thermos with a good strong coffee like **Trinidad** ☀ or
  Haitian ☀ for a real eye-opener

I use **Seasoned Sea Salt** ☀ in most recipes (except sweet
or dessert ones). It is all natural and the additional herbs and
spices in this seasoning enhance recipe flavour with a reduced
amount of salt.

5

Daybreak on Deck à Deux

Rise and Shine!

A peaceful and intimate time

to share and to contemplate

the day ahead.

Heart Starter

Sausage & Cheese Gratin

Toasted Herbal "Roll-Ups"

Coffee

Tea

Serves 2-6

Heart Starter

Here's lookin' at you, Ed

For each drink:
2 oz. vodka
3 oz. cranberry juice
3 oz. freshly squeezed orange juice
1/2 tsp. **Sorrel Syrup** ☀
crushed ice

1 oz. = 2 Tbs.

- Place all ingredients in a shaker.
- Shake until drink is well chilled.
- Serve in large goblet, garnished with orange slice and/or fresh mint.

Sausage and Cheese Gratin

1/2 c. finely chopped onions
3 cloves garlic, minced
2 Tbs. unsalted butter
2 Tbs. lite oil
1/2 c. crumbled, cooked sausage
  (or diced ham)
1/4 c. milk
4 eggs
1 tsp. **Mixed Hearty Herbs** ☀
1/4 tsp. **Seasoned Sea Salt** ☀
few grinds **Spiced Peppercorns** ☀
2/3 c. grated Swiss cheese
3 medium potatoes

* Mushrooms, green peppers are also a good addition.

☾ Potatoes may be grated ahead of time and held in a bowl of water in fridge.

- Preheat oven to 375°.
- Sauté onions and garlic in butter and oil until soft, not brown (about 5 minutes).
- Add sausage and cook slightly.
- In a bowl, beat eggs with milk.
- Add seasonings, and cheese.
- Blend in sausage and onions*.
- Peel and coarsely grate potatoes. ☾
- Squeeze water from potatoes and add to mixture in bowl.
- Pour into well buttered 9-11 inch baking or quiche dish.
- Bake for about 30 min. or until just firm and lightly browned.

≈ Leftovers make a wonderful cold snack or lunch. The Gratin also packs well for a picnic or traveling.

Toasted Herbal "Roll Ups"

1 loaf "home-made style" thinly
   sliced bread
3/4 c. butter (1-1/2 sticks),
   or 3/4 c. lite margarine
2 – 3 tsp. **Mild Savory Herbs** ☀ *

* **Super Spice** ☀ or **Mixed Hearty
Herbs** ☀ are good variations.

- Preheat oven to 425°
- Mix **Mild Savory Herbs** ☀ with softened butter or margarine and let mellow.
- Trim crusts from bread.
- Roll bread slices flat with rolling pin (at least 2 at a time).
- Spread each slice with herbal butter-completely covering.
- Roll up and place, seam side down, on lightly buttered cookie sheet.
- Lightly brush top with melted butter or margarine.
- Bake for 10 min. turning after first 5 min. (or until brown).

≈ "Roll Ups" may be frozen before or after baking.

≈ Keep a supply in freezer for snacks or as a good accompaniment to a soup or salad lunch.

For maximum flavour, dried herbs and seasonings should be
hydrated with the liquid or moist ingredients of a recipe before
using (at least one half hour). Herbal butters, sauces, spreads
and dips all benefit from mellowing time.

Terrace Treat

A Special Day…a *special*

breakfast…for Mother's Day,

birthday, anniversary or

just because…

Tropical Honey Cup

Epicurean Ham & Asparagus

Savoury Island Hollandaise

Basque Tomatoes

Spiced Coffee with Plantation Sugar

Serves 4

Tropical Honey Cup

1/4 c. low fat yogurt or sour cream
2 tsp. **West Indian Honey** ☀
1 tsp. **Guavaberry Liqueur** ☀
freshly grated **Nutmeg**
2 oranges cut into sections
2 bananas sliced into 1/2 in. pieces
3 kiwi fruit peeled, halved lengthwise, and cut crosswise into
  1/2 in. pieces
  Strawberries, peaches, pineapple,
  blueberries, grapes, melon can be
  substituted according to seasonal availability.

- Whisk yogurt, **W.I. Honey** ☀, and
  Guavaberry Liqueur ☀ until
  smooth.
- Add fruit and gently mix until well
  coated.
- Chill until serving time.
- Grate light sprinkling of **Nutmeg**
  over each serving.
- Particularly colourful and appeal-
  ing served in cut glass bowls or
  crystal goblets.

≈ Any amount of fruit can be used. Adjust amount of dressing
  accordingly (it can be doubled).

Epicurean Ham and Asparagus

4 slices "homemade" style bread
4 servings ham
  Suggestions: Smithfield or
  Southern, Canadian bacon,
  boiled, country, smoked,
  Proscuitto, Parma
4 servings fresh asparagus
Savoury Island Hollandaise
  (see next page)

- Toast bread.
- Sauté ham until brown (except
  Prosciutto or Parma).
- Cook asparagus, uncovered (to
  maintain bright green colour)
  until just tender but firm.
- On each hot plate place ham on
  toast then arrange asparagus on
  top of ham.
- Loosely cover with foil to keep
  warm while making **Savoury
  Island Hollandaise.**
- Top each serving with
  Hollandaise and sprinkle with
  chopped parsley.

Savoury Island Hollandaise

3 egg yolks
1 Tbs. **Lime Vinegar** ☀
1/2 tsp. **West Indian Rum Peppers** ☀
1/4 tsp. **Seasoned Sea Salt** ☀
1/2 c. butter
1 tsp. **Mild Savory Herbs** ☀

- Blend egg yolks, **Lime Vinegar** ☀, **Rum Peppers** ☀, and **Seasoned Sea Salt** ☀ quickly in blender.
- Heat butter and **Mild Savory Herbs** ☀ to bubbly stage.
- Pour butter into egg yolk mix in a steady stream while blending. When all butter is added, sauce is done.

Basque Tomatoes

2 medium tomatoes
dash of **Seasoned Sea Salt** ☀
1/2 c. **Herbal Bread Crumbs***
2 Tbs. finely chopped onion, scallion, or shallot
1/2 tsp. oil

- Preheat oven to 450°
- Scoop pulp from tomatoes.
- Lightly sprinkle shells with **Seasoned Sea Salt** ☀.
- Mix pulp with **Herbal Bread Crumbs**, onion, and oil.
- Place tomatoes in baking dish and bake for about 10 minutes, or until top is golden.
- Do not overcook tomatoes. If **Crumbs** are not brown when tomatoes are done, then quickly brown under broiler.

≈ Stale bread put through food processor makes great crumbs.

*Herbal Bread Crumbs
- Combine 2 c. dry bread crumbs* and 6 tbs. **Presto Pesto** ☀.
Refrigerate leftover crumbs for other uses:
   1. Casserole toppings,
   2. Other stuffed veggies: onions, zucchini, eggplant
   3. Coating for fried meat or fish
   4. Meatloaf/meatball mix.

Sunny Side Up

A *"hot"* and hearty breakfast

with *South of the Border gusto,*

for *any* place or *any* season.

Broiled Grapefruit

Huevos Criollos

(Hash, poached eggs, salsa, sour cream and cheese)

Toast with Pepper Jelly

Spice Island Cocoa

Coffee

Serves 6

Broiled Grapefruit

3 grapefruit
2 Tbs. melted butter
1/2 c. **Sugar 'N' Spice** ☀

- Cut 3 grapefruit into halves.
- Mix butter and **Sugar 'N' Spice** ☀.
- Sprinkle mixture equally over halves.
- Broil until hot and bubbly.

Serves 6

Huevos Criollos

poached eggs on spicy hash with **Salsa**, sour cream, and cheese

Step I: Hash

1–16 oz. can corned beef hash
1–12 oz. can corned beef
3 Tbs. dry bread crumbs
3 Tbs. chopped onion
3 Tbs. chopped green pepper
2 Tbs. **Jerk Seasoning** ☀ (green)
   or 1-1/2 Tbs. **Kuchela** ☀

Step I:

- Mix all ingredients in Step 1 well.
- Shape into 6 large flat or 12 small flat patties.
- Place in greased pan.
- Broil both sides until brown and crispy.

Step II: Eggs

12 eggs

Step II:

- Quickly poach eggs*. (see next page)

Step III: Prepared Salsa

   (see p. 76)
sour cream
grated cheddar cheese

Step III:

- Place 1 egg on each pattie (or 2 on large pattie).
- Top egg with about 1 Tbs. **Salsa** and dollop of sour cream.
- Lightly sprinkle with grated cheese.

No Problem Poached Eggs

1. Put 1 Tbs. vinegar in skillet containing about 2 in. water.
2. Bring water to simmer.
3. Break eggs, one at a time, into small sauce dish and gently slip into simmering water.
4. Simmer for 3-5 minutes (spooning water over yolks) until whites are set but yolk is still very soft.
5. Remove eggs, in order of placement, with slotted spoon to pan of cold water (to stop cooking and rinse vinegar).
6. Trim white strands or uneven edges and refigerate in shallow bowl of fresh water until ready to use.
7. When ready to serve: Place eggs in very hot water for about 30 seconds. Blot dry on towel and serve immediately.

≋ This method takes away the worry of last minute timing, breaking yolks, or over cooking.

Spice Island Cocoa

2 oz. **Spice Island Cocoa Balls** ☀*
1 c. water
3 Tbs. **Sugar 'N' Spice** ☀
dash salt
3 c. milk

Variation
   Mocha chocolate:
   substitute 1 c. strong coffee for water

* 1 ball usually equals 1 oz.

- Coarsely grate **Cocoa Balls** ☀ into saucepan.
- Add 1 c. water and cook, stirring constantly, over low heat until grated **Cocoa Balls** ☀ are melted.
- Stir in **Sugar 'N' Spice** ☀ and salt.
- Bring to a boil, reduce heat, simmer for 5 min.
- Gradually add milk and heat without boiling.
- Top with marshmallow or whipped cream if desired.

Sunshine
Snack Attack

Courtside Coolers

Time out for a refreshing,

cooling "pick me up."

"The Famous" Coffee Cake

Curry Chutney Cheese
with fruit slices

or

Lisa's Curried Cheese Paté

Iced Caribbee Spiced Tea

California Coffee Coolers

"The Famous" Coffee Cake

For as long as I can remember this Coffee Cake was our traditional Christmas morning treat as well as being a holiday gift to friends. One of the children named it **"The Famous"**, for whatever reason, and it has been called that ever since. It is quick and easy enough to be a treat any time.

Step I: Batter
3/4 c. shortening
1-1/2 c. sugar
3 eggs
1 tsp. **Vanilla-Vanilla** ☀
3 c. flour
1-1/2 tsp. baking powder
1-1/2 tsp. baking soda
1-1/2 c. sour cream (lite)

Step II: Sugar 'N' Spice Mix
1/2 c. **Sugar 'N' Spice** ☀
1 c. chopped walnuts or pecans

Step I:

- Preheat oven to 350°.
- In a large bowl cream together shortening and sugar.
- Add eggs, one at a time, beating after each addition.
- Add **Vanilla-Vanilla** ☀ and mix.
- In separate bowl mix flour, baking powder, and baking soda.
- Alternately add flour mix and sour cream to sugar and shortening until all is well blended.

Step II:

- Mix **Sugar 'N' Spice** ☀ with nuts.
- Put half of the batter into a greased and floured tube pan.
- Sprinkle **Sugar 'N' Spice** ☀ mixture over batter and cover with remaining batter.
- Bake approx. 50 minutes.
- Cool, in pan, for 5-10 minutes before inverting onto cooling rack.

〰 This coffee cake keeps well in fridge and can be frozen.

Curry Chutney Cheese

Serve with apple, pear or melon slices. Also good with celery and assorted crackers

8 oz. cream cheese (lite)
2 Tbs. **Caribbee Curry** ☀
4 Tbs. **Sunny Caribbee Chutney** ☀
optional: 1/4 c. chopped nuts

- Mix all ingredients. (If chutney is in large pieces: Mash with fork or in food processor.)
- Chill for 24 hours for best blending of flavours.

≋ For a veggie dip: Thin with yogurt or milk and adjust amount of curry.

Lisa's Curried Cheese Paté

This version of similar flavours is so good, that I had to give you a choice !

10 oz. grated Sharp Cheddar Cheese
8 oz. cream cheese (lite)
2 Tbs. **Caribbee Curry** ☀
Sunny Caribbee Chutney ☀
1/2 c. finely chopped scallions

- Blend first three ingredients well.
- Press mixture into a small loaf pan lined with plastic wrap.
- Refrigerate for at least 8 hours.
- Turn onto a serving plate and top with **Sunny Caribbee Chutney** ☀.
- Edge plate with scallions.
- Serve at room temperature with crackers.

Use lite or low fat, low cholesterol or reduced calorie dairy products in recipes, unless otherwise stated. Good quality oils, margarine, mayonnaise, milk, yogurt, sour cream, cream cheese, cottage cheese are all available "Lite". Feta and Chèvre cheese are low fat as are some brands of Ricotta and Mozzarella. Read the labels. Low fat sour cream and yogurt are sometimes more "sour" and thinner in consistency depending on brand. Adjust recipes accordingly. If a recipe calls for real butter or extra virgin olive oil it is because the flavour of these is essential for that recipe.

California Coffee Coolers

1 qt. water
1/4 c. **California Coffee Mix***
Spice Island Cocoa Ball ☀
Nutmeg

***California Coffee Mix**
1/2 c. instant coffee
1/2 c. **Sugar 'N' Spice** ☀
Mix and store in covered container

- In pitcher add 1 c. hot water to 1/4 c. **California Coffee Mix***.
- Mix well until coffee mix dissolves.
- Add remaining 3 c. water.
- Pour over ice into individual tall glasses.
- Add cream to taste or garnish with dollop of whipped cream and grated **Spice Island Cocoa Ball** ☀ or **Nutmeg**.

Iced Caribbee Spiced Tea

1 qt. water
1/4 c. **Caribbee Spiced Tea** ☀

- In a pitcher, add 1 c. hot water to **Caribbee Spiced Tea** ☀.
- Mix well until "**Tea**" is dissolved.
- Add remaining 3 c. cold water.
- Pour over ice into individual glasses.
- Garnish with orange or lemon slices.

Measurement Equivalents

1 teaspoon	=	1/3 tablespoon
1 tablespoon	=	3 teaspoons
2 tablespoons	=	1 fluid ounce
4 tablespoons	=	1/4 cup or 2 ounces
5-1/3 tablespoons	=	1/3 cup or 2-2/3 ounces
8 tablespoons	=	1/2 cup or 4 ounces
16 tablespoons	=	1 cup or 8 ounces
1/4 cup	=	4 tablespoons
3/8 cup	=	1/4 cup plus 2 tablespoons
5/8 cup	=	1/2 cup plus 2 tablespoons
7/8 cup	=	3/4 cup plus 2 tablespoons
1 cup	=	1/2 pint or 8 fluid ounces
2 cups	=	1 pint or 16 fluid ounces
1 pint, liquid	=	16 fluid ounces
1 quart, liquid	=	2 pints or 4 cups
1 gallon, liquid	=	4 quarts

Butter, 1 stick	= 4 ounces	=	8 tablespoons or 1/2 cup
4 sticks	= 1 lb.	=	2 cups
whipped, 6 sticks	= 1 lb.	=	3 cups
Cheese, dry	1 lb.	=	4 cups
freshly shredded	1/4 lb.	=	1 cup
Chocolate	1 ounce	=	1 square or 4 tablespoons grated
Cream, whipping	1 cup unwhipped	=	2 to 2-1/2 cups whipped
Eggs			
extra large	4	=	1 cup
large	5	=	1 cup
medium	6	=	1 cup
small	7	=	1 cup
Flour			
cake	1 lb.	=	4-3/4 cups
white, all purpose	1 lb.	=	4 cups
Potatoes	1 lb.	=	3 medium-sized
Rice	1 lb. or 2 cups uncooked	=	6 cups cooked
Sugar, granulated	1 lb.	=	2 cups
brown, packed	1 lb.	=	2-1/4 cups
confectioners'	1 lb.	=	3-1/2 to 4 cups
Walnuts, English	2 to 2-1/2 lbs. in shell	=	1 lb. shelled or 4-1/4 cups halves
Yeast, active dry	1 package	=	1 tablespoon

All measurements are approximate in that they have been rounded off to the nearest measure.

Dockside Delacacies

Working on the boat, catching

fish or water skiing makes us

hungry and thirsty.

Florentine Spinach Squares

Ham & Cheese Crescents

Cajun Fish Fix

Mango Sun Tea

Florentine Spinach Squares

4 tbs. butter
3 eggs
1 c. flour
1 tsp. baking powder
1 tsp. **Seasoned Sea Salt** ☀
1 Tbs. **Presto Pesto** ☀
1/2 tsp. **Herb Pepper** ☀
3/4 c. milk (low fat)
12 oz. Monterey Jack cheese
2 packs frozen, chopped spinach,
    drained and squeezed dry

≋   These freeze well.

Makes 48–60 1-1/4 to 1-1/2 inch small squares.

- Preheat oven to 350°.
- In oven, melt butter in 9x13 baking pan.
- In large bowl beat eggs.
- Add flour, baking powder, seasonings, and milk, mixing well.
- Add cheese and spinach and mix well.
- Pour into buttered pan.
- Bake about 35 minutes or until lightly browned and springy to touch.
- Remove from oven and cool before cutting into squares.

Ham and Cheese Crescents

1 tube refrigerated crescent
    dinner rolls*
Island Nutmeg Mustard ☀
    (prepared)
Finely chopped ham (or thin slices)
Shredded cheddar, provolone,
    or swiss cheese
Chutney ☀ (mango or papaya)

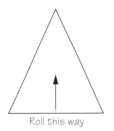

Roll this way

*Sandwich bread, crusts removed,
rolled thin can be substituted.
See p.9

- Preheat oven to 375°.
- Separate dough into triangles.
- *Lightly spread* **Island Nutmeg Mustard** ☀ on each triangle.
- Place small amount chopped ham (or thin slice) on each triangle.
- Sprinkle with cheese (about 1-1/2 tsp.).
- Put about 1/2 tsp. **Chutney** ☀ in middle of triangle.
- Roll up, starting at short end of triangle and roll towards opposite point.
- Place roll, pointside down, on greased baking sheet. (Curve ends into crescent shape.)
- Bake for 10-13 min. or until brown.

Cajun Fish Fix

2 c. roasted salted nuts
1 c. golden raisins
4 c. corn chips
2 c. Chex cereal
1 c. pretzel sticks
1/2 c. unsalted butter, melted
1 Tbs. plus 1 tsp. **Island Fish Spice** ☀
1-1/2 tsp. **Garlic Powder**

- Preheat oven to 250°.*
- In large bowl combine nuts, raisins, corn chips, Chex and pretzels.
- Add **Island Fish Spice** ☀ and **Garlic Powder** to melted butter and mix well.
- Pour seasoned butter over nut mixture and lightly but thoroughly toss until evenly coated.
- Bake on large cookie sheet for 1 hour, stirring every 15 minutes.

*Accurate oven temperature is essential. Too hot an oven will burn the "Fix".

Mango Sun Tea

The **Sun Tea** method of making "Iced Tea" produces a clearer drink.

1/4 c. **Sunny Caribbee Mango Tea** ☀ (or any flavour)
2 qts. water

* Can add sugar here if desired. I use 1 or 2 packets "pink sugar" or some **West Indian Honey** ☀ to sweeten, with fewer calories

- Place tea in 2 quart covered jar.
- Place jar in sun for a day (or until colour and flavour is rich).
- Strain into serving pitcher.*
- Serve over ice in tall glasses garnished with orange or lemon slices.

Lounge Lizards' Libations

Chill out.

Watch the clouds go by.

Read, day dream, snack and nap.

Have a long cold drink and enjoy

doing not much of anything.

It's Nuttin' Honey

Crab Puffs

Crudités with Pesto Power Dip

Sorrel Swizzle

It's "Nuttin' Honey"

1-1/2 c. sugar
1/4 tsp. salt
1/4 c. **West Indian Honey** ☀
1/2 c. water
3 cups pecan halves
1/2 tsp. **Vanilla-Vanilla** ☀

- Combine sugar, salt, **West Indian Honey** ☀, and water in medium sauce pan.
- Cook over medium heat, stirring constantly, until sugar is dissolved.
- Continue to cook without stirring until candy thermometer reads 244° (or until soft ball forms in cold water).
- Remove pan from heat; add nuts and **Vanilla-Vanilla** ☀.
- Stir gently until mix becomes creamy.
- Turn onto waxed paper, separating nuts with fork.

Crab Puffs

1/2 c. boiling water
1/4 c. butter
1/2 c. flour
2 eggs
1/2 tsp. **Island Fish Spice** ☀
1/2 tsp. **Mild Savory Herbs** ☀
1/2 c. crabmeat*

*can replace with grated cheese
**can be frozen in zip locked bags. Quickly crisp puffs in hot oven before serving

- Preheat oven to 400°.
- In saucepan, melt butter in boiling water.
- Add flour and cook, stirring vigorously, until batter forms a ball.
- Remove from heat and cool slightly.
- Add eggs, one at a time, beating well after each addition until batter is smooth.
- Add crabmeat and seasonings; mix well.
- Drop batter by half teaspoonsful onto greased baking sheet.
- Bake for about 20 min., or until golden brown and crisp.
- Make small prick in each to let steam escape and cool on rack.**

Pesto Power Dip

1/2 c. mayonnaise (lite)
1/2 c. sour cream (lite)
1-1/2 to 2 Tbs. **Presto Pesto** ☀

- Combine all ingredients and let mellow several hours.
- Serve with Crudités:
  Celery sticks, carrot sticks, radishes, broccoli and cauliflower "flowerettes", zucchini or cucumber sticks, mushrooms, Belgian endive leaves.

≈ Serve in a Bell Pepper Serving "Bowl"

Sorrel Swizzle

A colourful and refreshing drink

1 to 2 Tbs. **Sorrel Syrup** ☀
8 oz. water or club soda

- In a tall glass mix **Sorrel Syrup** ☀ and water or club soda (soda is best).
- Add ice and garnish with lemon slice.

≈ Add vodka or rum for a festive cocktail.

Brilliant Brunches

Sunny Sunday Brunch

It's the first warm day of spring or a sparkling fall morning "before the game." We'll get out the grill and have a robust repast…
a Mediterranean version of the traditional "mixed grill".

Bloody Bulls Olé

Lamburgers David

Chops Taverna Style

Provençal Eggs

Green Beans Vinaigrette

Serves 8

Bloody Bulls Olé

For each 10 oz glass:
1-1/2 – 2 oz. vodka
1/2 tsp. **Bloody Mary Magic** ☀
1 tsp. lemon or lime juice
3 – 4 oz. beef bouillon
2 – 3 oz. V-8 or tomato juice
3 – 4 dashes **West Indian Rum Peppers** ☀

- Thoroughly mix or shake all ingredients.
- Fill glass with ice.
- Garnish with celery stick or cucumber slice.

Variation: Serve this hot, in mugs, on a cold winter day or carry, in a thermos, to a tailgate picnic.

Lamburgers David

To open the door to David's refrigerator is to view "Condiment City". The vast and mysterious array of boxes, bottles and jars is the heart and soul of his copius culinary adventures.

2 lbs. ground lamb
2 Tbs. **Jerk Seasoning** ☀ (green) or
   1-1/2 Tbs. **Kuchela** ☀
1 tsp. **Seasoned Sea Salt** ☀
1/2 tsp. crushed **Rosemary**

- Mix all ingredients well.
- Form into desired size patties:
  1. Makes 16 sausage type patties for brunch or breakfast.
  2. Makes 8 lunch size patties.
- Cook, according to size, until preferred doneness (medium-medium rare is best).

Chops Taverna Style

16 1-1/4 inch thick lamb loin chops
   (2 per person)
1 Tbs. **Mixed Hearty Herbs** ☼
2-1/4 tsp. **Seasoned Sea Salt** ☼
2-1/4 tsp. **Herb Pepper** ☼
2 Tbs. garlic, minced
1-1/2 Tbs. lemon juice
1-1/2 Tbs. olive oil

- Combine all ingredients to make
  a paste.
- Rub chops with paste and let
  marinate at room temperature
  for several hours or overnight in
  fridge.
- Broil in oven or on grill (4 inches
  from heat) 4 – 5 min. for
  medium-rare (use meat
  thermometer).

Garlic is an omnipotent ingredient in "Cuisines of the Sun"
particularly in countries bordering the Mediterranean: Spain,
Italy, France, and Portugal. The cuisines, indigenous to these
countries, are pungent and robust and characterize their
culture and heritage.

Historically, Garlic has been considered a miracle cure for
centuries. It's healing qualities, in treatments of colds, asthma,
arthritis, diarreah, diabetes, heart disease (to name a few)
have been extolled through out the world.

It is also claimed that garlic has supernatural powers. Worn
around the neck, Garlic repels numerous enemies including
Vampires, evil eye, warlocks and sorcerers and attracts love,
good luck and enhances fertility.

Provençal Eggs

For each serving:

1 medium (3 – 3-1/2 in.) firm, ripe
   tomato

Seasoned Sea Salt ☀

Herb Pepper ☀

1/4 tsp. **Presto Pesto** ☀

1 egg

1/2 tsp. **Herbal Bread Crumbs**
   (see p. 13)

- Preheat oven to 350°.
- Cut small slice from top of tomato.
- Scoop out seeds and pulp.
- Sprinkle shell lightly with salt and drain upsidedown on rack or paper towel for a few minutes.
- Place tomato, rightside up, in buttered pan-preferrably a small Ramekin.
- Sprinkle with dash of **Seasoned Sea Salt** ☀ and **Herb Pepper** ☀ and 1/4 tsp. **Presto Pesto** ☀.
- Place egg in shell.
- Bake for 20-25 minutes or until egg just set – do not overcook.
- Sprinkle 1/2 tsp. **Herbal Bread Crumbs** on top.
- Pass under broiler quickly to brown crumbs.

Green Beans Vinaigrette

Dressing:
3 Tbs. extra virgin olive oil
1 Tbs. Balsamic vinegar
1 tsp. **Mild Savory Herbs** ☀
1/4 tsp. **Seasoned Sea Salt** ☀
freshly ground **Spiced Peppercorns** ☀ (to taste)
1/4 tsp. Dijon mustard
1 large clove garlic, minced

1-1/4 lb. fresh, crisp medium green
  beans

- Combine all dressing ingredients in covered jar. Shake well to mix and let sit for several hours before using.

- Add beans to large pot of boiling salted water.
- Cover pot until water returns to boil.
- Cook beans, <u>uncovered</u>, 4-5 minutes or until tender but crunchy.
- Drain and immediately immerse in pot of ice water, to stop cooking.
- Drain again and dry in a cloth or paper towels.
- 20 – 25 minutes before serving toss beans with dressing. Chill.*

*Marinating for too long will destroy bright green colour

≈ For full flavoured salad dressings, it is advantageous to let dry seasoning steep in vinegar for 10 to 15 minutes before adding oil. Dressings improve with room temperature sitting time.

Summer Celebration

Gather family and friends for

an easy and elegant buffet…

a salute to summer !

Morning Madras

Ginger Rum Ham

Neapolitan Noodles

Curried Fruit Savannah

Herbal Pita Crisps

Dixie Daisies

Serves 12 – 14

Morning Madras

For each serving:
1-1/2 – 2 oz. vodka
4 oz. freshly squeezed orange juice
1 Tbs. **Sorrel Syrup** ☀

- Pour vodka and juice over ice into large glass or goblet.
- Float **Sorrel Syrup** ☀ slowly on top.
- Garnish with orange slice and/or sprig of mint.

Ginger Rum Ham

7 – 8 lb. cooked-cured ham
1/4 c. Crystallized **Ginger Gems** ☀
  (finely chopped)
1/4 c. **Ginger Beer Syrup** ☀
3 Tbs. **Sugar 'N' Spice** ☀
3 Tbs. dark rum
1 tsp. **Island Nutmeg Mustard** ☀
  (prepared)

- Preheat oven to 350°.
- Remove skin from ham, leaving about 1/3 inch layer of fat.
- Score fat into diamonds.
- Combine all ingredients to make glaze.
- Spread glaze over all.
- Bake ham for 55 minutes.

Neapolitan Noodles

12 oz. package thin noodles
16 oz. cottage cheese (lite)
16 oz. sour cream (lite)
1/2 c. milk
3 Tbs. **Down Island Dill** ☀
1 tsp. **Seasoned Sea Salt** ☀
few grinds **Spiced Peppercorns** ☀
6 scallions thinly sliced
   (whites and a little green)
1 lg. clove garlic minced
1/4 c. fresh parsley chopped
   (or abour 4 tsp. dried)
1/2 c. grated sharp cheddar cheese
1/2 c. grated parmesan cheese
unsalted butter

- Preheat oven to 350°.
- Cook noodles according to package directions.
- Drain noodles.
- While noodles are still warm combine with remaining ingredients with the exception of cheddar and parmesan cheese.
- Place in large, shallow, buttered baking dish.
- Sprinkle with combined cheeses and dot with butter.
- Bake for 40 minutes or until hot throughout and golden crunchy on top.

Serves 10-12

Curried Fruit Savannah

1 lg. can peaches
1 lg. can apricots
1 lg. can pears
1 med. can pineapple chunks
1 c. white raisins
1/2 c. brown sugar
1/4 c. **Sugar 'N' Spice** ☀
1/3 c. butter, melted
1 Tbs. **Caribbee Curry** ☀

- Preheat oven to 325°.
- Drain fruit.
- Combine sugars and **Caribbee Curry** ☀ with butter.
- Place fruit in casserole.
- Pour **Caribbee Curry** ☀, butter and sugar mixture over fruit.
- Bake, uncovered, for 1 hour. ☾

☾ Can be made ahead. Reheat at 325° until hot.

Herbal Pita Crisps

3/4 c. softened butter or
  margarine
1/4 grated parmesan cheese
1 – 2 cloves garlic, minced
2 – 3 tsp. **Mixed Hearty Herbs** ☀
Six (7 inch) pita bread

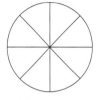

Cut with pizza cutter

- Preheat oven to 375°.
- Cream first 4 ingredients
  together.
- Split pitas.
- Spread rough side of pitas lightly
  with butter mix.
- Cut into pie shaped wedges (8)
  and place on baking sheet.
- Bake for about 8-10 min. or until
  crisp and golden brown.

☾ These may be made ahead and frozen or kept in covered tin.
  Reheat to crisp.

Dixie Daisies

1 stick margarine (not butter)
1/4 c. sugar
1 c. flour
Sunny Caribbee Jelly ☀
  Passionfruit
  Guava
Nutmeg

IMPORTANT:
  use margarine, not butter;
  use jelly, not jam

- Preheat oven to 375°.
- Cream margarine and sugar.
- Stir in flour and mix well.
- Form into small balls about 1 inch
  in diameter.
- Place on ungreased baking sheet.
- Make an indentation in each ball
  with little finger.
- Fill indentation with **Sunny
  Caribbee Jelly** ☀ (about 1/4 tsp.).
- Bake for 8-10 minutes until
  slightly firm and lightly brown.
Makes about 2 dozen Daisies.

Metric Conversion

Liquid Measurements

1 tablespoon	= 1 ounce	= 1/4 deciliter	1-2/3 cups	= 13-1/3 ounces	= 3-3/4 deciliters
1/4 cup or	= 2 ounces	= 1/2 deciliter	1-3/4 cups	= 14 ounces	= 4 deciliters
4 tablespoons			2 cups or	= 16 ounces	= 1/2 liter
1/3 cup	= 2-2/3 ounces	= 3/4 deciliter	1 pint		
1/2 cup	= 4 ounces	= 1 deciliter	2-1/2 cups	= 20 ounces	= 6 deciliters
2/3 cup	= 5-1/3 ounces	= 1-1/2 deciliters	3 cups	= 24 ounces	= 3/4 liter
3/4 cup	= 6 ounces	= 1-3/4 deciliters	3-1/2 cups	= 28 ounces	= 4/5 liter or
1 cup	= 8 ounces	= 1/4 liter			8 deciliters
1-1/4 cups	= 10 ounces	= 3 deciliters	4 cups or	= 32 ounces	= 1 liter
1-1/3 cups	= 10-2/3 ounces	= 3-1/4 deciliters	1 quart		
1-1/2 cups	= 12 ounces	= 3-1/2 deciliters	A deciliter equals 1/10 liter.		

Solid Measures

1 ounce		= 30 grams	12 ounces	= 3/4 lb.	= 340 grams
2 ounces		= 60 grams	14 ounces		= 400 grams
3 ounces		= 85 grams	16 ounces	= 1 lb.	= 450 grams
4 ounces	= 1/4 lb.	= 115 grams	18 ounces	= 1-1/8 lb.	= 500 grams or
5 ounces		= 140 grams			1/2 kilogram
6 ounces		= 180 grams	20 ounces	= 1-1/4 lb.	= 560 grams
8 ounces	= 1/2 lb.	= 225 grams	24 ounces	= 1-1/2 lb.	= 675 grams
9 ounces		= 250 grams or	28 ounces	= 1-3/4 lb.	= 800 grams
		1/4 kilogram	32 ounces	= 2 lbs.	= 900 grams
10 ounces		= 285 grams		2-1/4 lbs	= 1000 grams or
					1 kilogram

Temperatures

Fahrenheit°		Celcius°/Centigrade°	Fahrenheit°		Celcius°/Centigrade°
0		-17	212	water boils	100
32	water freezes	0	250-275	very low oven	121-133
100		38	300-325	low oven	149-163
115	water simmers	46	350-325	moderate oven	177-190
130	water scalds	54	400-425	hot oven	204-218
150		66	450-475	very hot oven	232-246
200		95	500-525	extremely hot oven	260-274

All measurements are approximate in that they have been rounded off to the nearest measure.

Regatta Watch

We'll fill our picnic baskets and

coolers, find a perfect viewing spot,

spread the festive cloth and await

the thrilling contest.

Gutsy Gazpacho

Jamaican Drums

Carnival Crunch

Pesto Crostini

Fruit Kabobs

Serves 6

Gutsy Gazpacho

1 – 2 crushed garlic cloves
1 medium red pepper
1 medium green pepper
1 medium red onion
1 cucumber-seeded
2 lg. stalks celery
    (strings removed)
1 16 oz. can tomatoes,
    or 5 – 6 peeled fresh
1/4 c. olive oil
1/2 c. **Hot Pepper Vinegar** ☀ *
2 c. tomato or V-8 juice
3 Tbs. **Sunshine Salsa** ☀ (dry mix)
1 tsp. **Seasoned Sea Salt** ☀
1 tsp. **Herb Pepper** ☀

* Substitute:
    Red wine vinegar and dash
    Caribbee HotSauce ☀ or **West
    Indian Rum Peppers** ☀.

- Coarsly chop garlic, vegetables and tomatoes in food processor.
- Add vinegar and oil.
- Whirl again, leaving veggies quite coarse.
- Separately, combine 1 c. juice with 3 Tbs. **Sunshine Salsa** ☀ and let sit a few minutes to soften.
- Add Salsa and juice mix to veggie mix and whirl again.
- Add veggie mix and remaining 1 c. juice to large container.
- Add **Seasoned Sea Salt** ☀ and **Herb Pepper** ☀.
- Cover and chill for several hours.
- Garnish with dollop sour cream or yogurt, chopped chives and parsley.

Makes approximatley six 8 oz. servings.

≈ If soup too fiery or thick – add more juice and adjust **Seasoned Sea Salt** ☀ and **Herb Pepper** ☀.

Bring chilled or frozen food to *cool* room temperature before serving. Soups and salads, particularly, may lose some flavour with chilling. Taste and re-adjust seasonings before serving,

Jamaican Drums

3 lbs. chicken drumsticks (about 18 medium)
1 Tbs. oil
1/2 c. **Jerk Sauce** ☀
2 cloves garlic, minced
1-1/4 c. water
Jerk Spice ☀ (dry)

- Mix **Jerk Sauce** ☀, oil, and garlic in a ziplock bag.
- Place drumsticks in bag, close tightly and marinate for at least 1 hour.
- Place chicken, marinade and water in a large pot.
- Simmer, covered, over very low heat, stirring occasionally, for 1 – 1-1/2 hours, or until very tender.
- Remove from sauce.
- Sprinkle **Jerk Spice** ☀ on each drumstick.
- Grill, turning once, until brown and crispy.*

*These can be held, covered with foil in low heat oven for long time

Use ziplock bags for marinating or "crumbing" for thorough and even coverage with no mess and no fuss !

Carnival Crunch

Marinated, colourful, crisp seasonal vegetables

Your choice: Red, yellow, orange, or
green peppers, cucumber,
zucchini chunks, celery, radishes,
cauliflower, blanched broccoli or
brussel sprouts, red onion,
cherry tomatoes
sliced scallions

Marinade:
Simple Super Salad Dressing*
1/4 c. vinegar (**Lemon Grass** ☀,
   Hot Pepper ☀, or your favourite)
3/4 c. vegetable oil
3 tsp. **Super Spice** ☀
Mix all in covered jar and shake well
   to blend.

- Cut your vegetable choices into
  1 – 2 inch pieces so that they can
  be eaten as "finger food".**
- Place in large bowl and add sliced
  scallions.
- Cover with marinade (salad
  dressing) and marinate for at
  least several hours (mixing
  occasionally).

***Mild Savoury Vinaigrette** is a good alternative (see p. 159)

** Your choice of veggies cut into finer dice (1/2 inch) makes a good side salad.

〰 Whirl leftover veggies or salad in food processor, adding V-8 or
   tomato juice and adjusting seasonings for an instant **Gazpacho**.

Pesto Crostini

French or Italian bread
extra virgin olive oil*
Presto-Pesto ☀

* It is important to use full
   flavoured extra virgin olive oil for
   best results

- Preheat oven to 350°.
- Cut bread into 1/4 inch slices.
- Place slices on baking sheet.
- Brush each slice with olive oil.
- Sprinkle and spread **Presto-
  Pesto** ☀ on each slice.
- Bake for about 10 minutes until
  lightly browned and crisp.

Fruit Kabobs

Variety of ripe, colourful seasonal
    fruits:
melon balls (all types), whole
    strawberries, seedless grapes,
    3/4 inch banana slices or peach,
    apple or pineapple cubes, etc.
    (10-12 pieces per person)
1/3 c. mixed orange and lemon juice

Dipping Sauce:
1-1/2 c. sour cream
1/4 c. **Sugar 'N' Spice** ☀
1/2 c. **Guavaberry Liqueur** ☀

- Marinate cut fruit in juice, in
  covered bowl, and chill until ready
  to serve.
- When time to serve, thread 3 or
  4 pieces of fruit on each skewer
  (depending on skewer size).
- Serve Fruit Kabobs on platter
  garnished with mint and with bowl
  of Dipping Sauce.

- Mix dip ingredients and let
  flavours blend for at least an
  hour.
- Put in bowl large enough for
  dipping Kabobs.

Iced Lemon Spice Tea

Lemon Spice Tea ☀ is a refreshing, cooling accompaniment to this zesty brunch. Like all Iced Teas, it has no fat, sugar or calories and less caffeine than so called "soft drinks". Make it either the traditional or **Sun Tea** way (p. 29)

Traditional:
Steep 6 tsp. **Lemon Spice Tea** ☀ in 1 qt. boiling water for 5–10 minutes. Add ice and sweetener if desired.

Luscious Lunches

Picnic in Paradise

A portable "do ahead" treat

for easy transporting to any place

in your "paradise"… in the park,

by the pond, beneath the pines or

in your own backyard.

Carib☀bean Chili

Fog City Salad

Tex-Mex Corn Bread

Melon Medley

Spicee Sangria

Serves 8

Carib☀bean Chili

This universal favourite, transcending all ages, classes, cultures and climates is available in kit form at **Sunny Caribbee Spice Co.** Keep a few "kits" on your pantry shelf for last minute meals or unexpected guests – or do it yourself with this recipe.

2 c. mixed beans (your choice-
   kidney, navy, blackeyed, pinto,
   northern, pink)
28 oz. canned tomatoes
2 c. water
1 **Bouquet Garni** ☀
1 lb. ground beef
1 green pepper
1 onion
3 Tbs. **Sunshine Salsa** ☀
2 tsp. **Ground Cumin**
1 tsp. **Dried Garlic Chips**
1/2 tsp. **Fennel Seed**
Caribbee Hot Sauce ☀

* Can substitute chicken, pork,
   sausage, or partially cooked
   eggplant.

☾ Make day (or 2) before serving
   for full flavour.

- Prepare beans: Boil beans in 2-1/2 qts. of water for 3 minutes and set aside, covered, for 1 hour.
- Drain beans, place back in pot with canned tomatoes, 2 c. water and **Bouquet Garni** ☀.
- Simmer, covered, for 1-1/2 hours.
- While beans simmer, lightly brown hamburger* and coarsely chop onion and pepper.
- After 1-1/2 hours, add beef*, onions and pepper and all seasonings (except **Caribbee Hot Sauce** ☀).
- Simmer for about 45-60 minutes more or until beans are the right doneness for you.
- If "Chili" gets too dry, add more liquid (V-8 or bouillon) and adjust seasoning. ☾
- Remove **Bouquet Garni** ☀ and add **Caribbee Hot Sauce** ☀ until desired "fire" is achieved (or pass separately for individual use).
- Serve with white or brown rice. If desired pass bowls of sour cream, grated sharp cheddar or Monteray Jack cheese and sliced scallions to "top off" the **Chili**.

Makes approximately 8 (1 cup) servings

Fog City Salad

2 – 3 avocados
lemon juice
1 c. orange sections*
1 c. grapefruit sections*

Fog City Salad Dressing:
1/2 c. **Simple Super Salad
    Dressing** (p. 52)
1-1/2 Tbs. **West Indian Honey** ☀
1 Tbs. fresh orange juice
2 Tbs mayonnaise (lite)

salad greens
red onion
Poppy Seed

* Can use canned – but fresh
   is better

- Peel and cut avocados into
  1 – 1-1/2 inch cubes.
- In shallow bowl coat avocados
  with lemon juice (to keep from
  darkening)
- In covered glass jar: combine
  **Simple Super Salad Dressing,
  West Indian Honey** ☀, orange
  juice and mayonnaise and shake
  until well blended.
- Combine avocados and fruit in
  sealable bowl.
- Pour enough dressing over all to
  coat well.
- At serving time arrange fruit and
  avocado onto large plate of
  lettuce (preferably Bibb) or on
  individual plates.
- Garnish with very thin slices of red
  onion and sprinkle with **Poppy
  Seed**.

≈ For a picnic: prepare avocado, fruit and dressing in a tightly
   sealable container that can be transported. Have chilled lettuce and
   garnishes in separate containers. Let everyone assemble their own
   salad, at picnic time.

Tex-Mex Corn Bread

1 c. corn meal*
1 c. flour
1 Tbs. sugar
2 tsp. baking powder
1 tsp **BBQ Seasoning** ☀
2 eggs, beaten
2/3 c. milk
1 Tbs. **Sunshine Salsa** ☀
1 c. sour cream
1/4 c. unsalted butter, melted
1 c. corn kernals (fresh, canned or frozen)
1 c. grated sharp cheddar cheese
1/4 c. thinly sliced scallion or finely chopped onion

* Coarse or stone ground is best.

- Preheat oven to to 375°.
- Mix first 5 ingredients well. Set aside.
- In separate bowl, beat eggs.
- Soften **Sunshine Salsa** ☀ in milk.
- Combine eggs, **Salsa** ☀ and milk, butter and sour cream with dry ingredients and mix well.
- Blend in the corn, cheese and scallions.
- Pour into greased 9x9 baking pan.
- Bake for 35 – 40 minutes or until golden brown and springy to touch.
- Cool in pan 10 minutes before cutting into squares.

≈ Squares can be split in half and toasted or used for small sandwich snacks.

60

Melon Medley

6 – 8 c. melon balls:* cantaloupe,
   honey dew, watermelon,
   cranshaw, casaba (according
   to availability and colour)
1/2 c. **Marmalade** , orange or
   grapefruit
1/4 c. orange juice
1 tsp. Crystallized **Ginger Gems** ,
   finely chopped
Mint garnish
optional: sour cream**

- Combine **Marmalade** , juice and
  Ginger Gems in a large bowl.
- Add melon balls and gently mix.
- Refrigerate until serving time.
- Garnish with small pieces of
  mint.

Serves 8

*A variety of colours and flavours makes this special.
**Sour cream may be folded in for a different version.

Spicee Sangria

2 Tbs. **Sugar 'N' Spice**
1 Tbs. **Sorrel Syrup**
1/3 c. water
juice of 1/2 orange
juice of 1/2 lemon
1 bottle red wine
sparkling water or club soda
bitters or **Mauby**

- In small pan combine first five
  ingredients.
- Heat to boiling and simmer,
  covered, for 5 minutes. Cool.
- Slice rind from orange and
  lemons.
- Add cooled juice mixture, rind and
  red wine to large pitcher.
- Chill.
- Before serving, add 10 oz.
  sparkling water.
- Dash of bitters or **Mauby** .

Poolside Panache

A splendid day for a splash party.

Bring your suit and your appetite …

we'll spend a cool and relaxing

afternoon by the pool.

"Cool as a Cucumber" Soup

Bouillabaise Salad à la Med
with Sauce Verte

Garlic Toast

Sabayon

Campari Caribe

Serves 6

"Cool as a Cucumber" Soup

(No-Cook Cooking)
1-1/2 c. chicken bouillon
1 tsp. **Dried Onion Chips**
1 tsp. **Garlic Chips**
4 – 5 large cucumbers
1 tsp. **West Indian Green** ☀
1 Tbs. **Down Island Dill** ☀
1 tsp. **Seasoned Sea Salt** ☀
1 pt. (16 oz.) yogurt or sour cream*

*I use lite.

**A "melon baller" speeds up this
job. Also great for scooping out
cherry tomatoes, peppers,
zucchini, as well as melons.

- In large bowl, soften **Onion Chips** and **Garlic Chips** in bouillon.
- Cut 8-10 thin slices from a cucumber (reserve in fridge).
- Peel, seed**, and chop remaining cucumber into chunks. Puree cucumber in food processor.
- Add bouillon, onion and garlic to cucumber in processor and whirl all until well mixed.
- Return cucumber mixture to bowl.
- Whisk in seasonings, **West Indian Green** ☀ and yogurt.
- Chill, covered, for several hours (the longer, the better).
- Ladle into goblets or bowls and garnish with cucumber slice, chopped chives, and finely minced radishes.

Makes 6 servings

Whenever possible, I use fresh onion, garlic, shallots and
scallions. However, you may substitute **Dried Onion Chips** or
Garlic Chips when you are out of fresh or in a hurry. It is
important to rehydrate "Chips" or flakes in a small amount of
liquid (before adding to recipe) to soften and release flavour.

1 Tbs. **Onion Chips** = 1/4 c. chopped raw onion
1/4 c. **Onion Chips** = 1 c. chopped raw onion
1/4 tsp. **Garlic Chips** = 1 **large** clove

Bouillabaise Salad à la Med

1 c. each: shrimp, lobster, chunk
   crab, poached scallops and/or
   white fish
2 tomatoes, cut into wedges
8 scallions, including greens,
   1/4 in. slices
8 pitted black olives, sliced
2 tsp. **Mild Savory Herbs** ☀
1/2 – 1 tsp. **Island Fish Spice** ☀

- In large bowl, toss seafood with **Island Fish Spice** ☀ and 1 tsp. **Mild Savory Herbs** ☀ to coat.
- Add tomatoes, scallions, olives and remaining **Mild Savory Herbs** ☀.
- Gently combine.
- In a large shallow serving bowl or platter, arrange all on a bed of mesclun* or mixed greens.**
- Serve **Sauce Verte** separately.

*Mesclun-specialty of Southern France: A variety of baby field greens
   such as Oak Leaf lettuce, Arugula, Chervil, Curly Endive, Radicchio,
   Escarole, Dandelion.

**Mixed greens: Romaine, Iceburg, Bibb, Watercress, Chinese Cabbage,
   Belgian Endive.

Sauce Verte

1-1/2 Tbs. **Lemon Grass Vinegar** ☀
1/2 tsp. **Mild Savory Herbs** ☀
1 tsp. **Down Island Dill** ☀
6 Tbs. finely minced parsley
2 tsp. minced capers
2 Tbs. thinly sliced scallions
1/2 tsp. minced garlic
1/2 c. mayonnaise (lite)
1/2 c. sour cream (lite)
1/2 tsp. **Seasoned Sea Salt** ☀
   (or to taste)
Lowfat milk or buttermilk

- Let **Mild Savory Herbs** ☀ and **Down Island Dill** ☀ hydrate in **Lemon Grass Vinegar** ☀ for 10 minutes.
- Prepare parsley, capers, scallions and garlic.*
- Add all to mayonnaise and sour cream.
- Let mellow for at least 1/2 hr.
- Thin to desired serving consistency with lowfat milk or buttermilk.
- Add **Seasoned Sea Salt** ☀.

* Finely minced spinach or watercress can also be added here for an even
   "greener sauce".

Grilled Garlic Toast

3/4 c. softened butter or
   margerine
1/4 c. grated parmesan cheese
1 – 2 cloves garlic, minced
2 – 3 tsp. **Mixed Hearty Herbs** ☀*

- Blend all ingredients and let mellow for 1/2 hour or more.
- Spread on French bread slices (covering to edges).
- Place under broiler until brown and bubbly.

* You can make tasty variations by using **Super Spice** ☀, **Caribbee Curry** ☀, (eliminate cheese) **Mild Savoury Herbs** ☀, **Presto Pesto** ☀, etc.

Sabayon

1 4.2 oz. pack vanilla pudding
1/4 c. dark rum
1 c. whipping cream
3 Tbs. finely minced, Crystallized
   Ginger Gems ☀
Nutmeg

- Prepare pudding according to package directions (using 1/4 c. less milk).
- Remove from heat and stir in rum.
- Chill, covered until almost set.
- Whip cream to soft peaks.
- Fold whipped cream mix and **Ginger Gems** ☀ into pudding.
- Refrigerate.
- Spoon into bowls.
- Sprinkle with **Ginger Gems** ☀ and grated **Nutmeg**.

6 servings

Campari Caribe

For each serving:
1 Tbs. or 1/2 oz. **Sorrel Syrup** ☀
Quinine water (tonic)
garnish

- Put **Sorrel Syrup** ☀ into tall 12 oz. glass.
- Add ice.
- Fill with Quinine.*
- Garnish with orange or lemon slice.

***Negril-Negroni:** Add 1-1/2 oz. vodka before adding Quinine.

Lazy Days of Summer

The forecast was hot and sunny.

We had "More than Mother's"

meatloaf for dinner and cooked

enough of everything to have a cool

and carefree lunch the next day.

Cheddar Chips Cha Cha Cha and Shandy

"More than Mother's" Meatloaf

South Beach Black Bean Salad

California Cucumbers

Jamaican Parfaits

Serves 6-8

Cheddar Chips Cha Cha Cha

Eight 6 inch Tortillas (soft)
2 Tbs. Vegetable Oil
1-1/2 tsp. **Jerk Spice** *
4 oz. shredded cheddar cheese

* **Fish Spice** is a good alternative seasoning for **Jerk Spice**

Keep oil and **Jerk Spice well mixed.

- Preheat oven to 375°.
- Mix oil and **Jerk Spice**.
- Brush oil mix on each tortilla (covering to edge)**.
- Cut each tortilla into 8 wedges (more if you want small chips) using pizza cutter.
- Place cut pieces onto baking sheet and sprinkle each with cheese.
- Bake until crisp and golden.

Shandy

1 chilled 12 oz. bottle of lite beer
12 oz. **Ginger Beer***
dash bitters or **Mauby**
grated **Nutmeg**

*Ginger Beer:
  2 – 3 Tbs. **Ginger Beer Syrup**
  12 oz. chilled club soda

- Pour equal amounts of **Ginger Beer** and lite beer into large frosted mugs.
- Add a dash of bitters or **Mauby** and grate a little **Nutmeg** on top.

Serves 2

"More than Mother's" Meatloaf

Make this recipe with low fat ground turkey and turkey sausage and enjoy guilt free second (or third!) helpings.

1/4 c. olive oil
1-1/2 c. finely diced onion
1/2 c. finely diced celery
3 cloves (about 1-1/2 tsp) minced garlic
2 eggs
3 Tbs. **Sunshine Salsa** ☀ (be sure to shake before measuring)
1/3 c. bread crumbs
1-1/2 lbs. ground beef (or turkey)
1 lb. hot italian sausage (or hot turkey sausage)
1/2 tsp. **Seasoned Sea Salt** ☀
1/4 c. minced fresh parsley or 4 tsp. dry
Spicee Catsup ☀

- Preheat oven to 350°.
- Sauté onion, celery and garlic in oil over moderate heat until tender.
- While vegetables are sauteeing, beat eggs in large bowl.
- Add **Sunshine Salsa** ☀ to eggs and let sit.
- Combine vegetables and oil with **Sunshine Salsa** ☀ and eggs in bowl.
- Add remaining ingredients and mix well.
- Form into 5" x 10" loaf in shallow baking pan.
- Glaze with **Spicee Catsup** ☀ before baking.
- Bake 1 – 1-1/4 hrs (or until meat thermometer reads 160°). Check after 1 hour.

Condiments:
  Spicee Catsup ☀, **Tangy Tropical Ting** ☀, **West Indian Green** ☀ or **Chutney** ☀

〰 Recipe is easily doubled - but bake in 2 loaves
  "More than Mother's" Meatloaf is terrific hot or cold:
1. As a main meat course with salads and/or vegetables.
2. For sandwiches: Slice thinly, spread **West Indian Green** ☀, **Spicee Catsup** ☀, or **Tangy Tropical Ting** ☀ on bread, top with lettuce, meatloaf and slices of onion.
3. For Appetizer: Serve as a "Country Pate" on lettuce garnished with capers, cornichons and **West Indian Green** ☀.

South Beach Black Bean Salad

The renaissance of South Miami Beach, with it's whimsical Art Deco District, has been accompanied by a new cuisine often referred to as "Floribbean". The exciting, boisterous, colorful rejuvenation of "Sobe" and its emerging dynamic cuisine, reflects the melting pot of Indian, Hispanic, Caribbean and "Soul" cultures that thrive in this trendsetting neighborhood.

1 lb. Black beans* (dry) or
  5 c. drained, canned
3/4 c. green pepper chopped 1/4
  inch dice
3/4 c. red pepper chopped 1/4 inch
  dice (medium size pepper will
  make about 3/4 c.)
1/2 c. red onion chopped 1/4 inch dice
3 large cloves garlic, minced
1/4 c. olive oil (lite)
2 Tbs. **Ginger Garlic Vinegar** ☀**
1 Tbs. **Spicee Catsup** ☀
2 tsp. **Jerk Spice** ☀
1 tsp. **Seasoned Sea Salt** ☀

1/4 c. chopped fresh parsley
2 Tbs. sliced scallion greens

Variation: **Lime Vinegar ☀

- Put beans into large serving bowl and add next 9 ingredients.
- Gently mix well and chill for several hours or overnight for more flavour.
- Mix in parsley and/or scallion greens before serving.
- Add more **Seasoned Sea Salt** ☀, if desired.

*To prepare **dry** beans:
- Boil beans in large amount of water for 2 minutes.
- Let sit for 1 hour covered.
- Drain and rinse (to de-gas).
- Return to pot with cold water.
- Bring to boil and simmer until tender but not mushy (should be quite firm).
- Drain and cool.

Mixed seasonings, as well as individual herbs and spices, have a varying shelf life. Keep all of these in a cool, dry place, tightly covered and out of bright light. If you have had your seasonings for a long time, some of the flavour value may be lost. In this case, you will have to adjust and increase the amount used.

California Cucumbers

4 large cucumbers
1 large red or Vidalia onion
1/4 c. **Hot Pepper Vinegar** ☀
1/4 c. white vinegar
1 tsp. **Seasoned Sea Salt** ☀
1 Tbs. **Down Island Dill** ☀

*The longer you marinate this (up
  to a week) the better the flavour

≈ This makes good relish or
  condiment as well as a salad.

- Peel, seed and chop cucumber into
  1/2 inch dice.
- Chop onion into about 1/4 inch dice.
- In large shallow bowl (or ziplock
  bag) combine cucumber, onion, **Hot
  Pepper Vinegar** ☀, **Seasoned Sea
  Salt** ☀ and **Down Island Dill** ☀.
- Refrigerate stirring or turning for
  at least several hours.*
- Drain and adjust seasoning as
  necessary.
- Serve on lettuce or mixed greens
  alone or with sliced tomatoes or
  sliced cooked beets.

Jamaican Parfaits or Sundaes

1 qt. coffee or vanilla ice cream
  (or frozen yogurt)
1/4 c. finely chopped Crystallized
  Ginger Gems ☀
Spice Island Chocolate Sauce
  (p. 169)

☾ Make ahead and keep on tray in
  freezer – covered with sheet of
  food wrap

Optional:
  Dark Rum may be added to
  sauce to taste

Serves 8

- Soften ice cream. Add **Ginger
  Gems** ☀ and mix well (reserve
  about 1 tsp. for garnish).
- Return to freezer to firm up.
- In 8 parfait glasses place about
  1 Tbs. **Chocolate Sauce**.
- Place large spoonful of ice cream
  in glass, pushing down to make
  sauce swirl up sides.
- Add more sauce and more ice
  cream.
- Finish with a bit of sauce and
  return to freezer. ☾
- About 15-20 minutes before
  serving, remove from freezer.
- Garnish with whipped cream and
  chopped **Ginger Gems** ☀.

Down Among the Sheltering Palms

The "cookout" has moved into the *nineties*. Pack up your hibachi, pick a cool spot and spice up the perennial classic with Caribbean pizazz.

Sunshine Salsa

Jamaican Jerk Burgers

Rasta Pasta

Sweet Potato "Ting"

Ginger Surprise

Mauby

Serves 8

Sunshine Salsa

3 – 4 Tbs. **Sunshine Salsa** ☀
16 oz. can of tomatoes
(chop tomatoes if pieces are
   large)

- Heat whole can of tomatoes just to simmer.
- Add **Sunshine Salsa** ☀.*
- Let mellow for at least 1/2 hour.
- Serve in a bowl surrounded by tortilla chips.

* Add more veggies if you want more crunch: Fine/medium dice scallions, peppers, onions, celery or cucumber

Jamaican Jerk Burgers

1 lb. ground turkey or beef*
1-1/2 – 2 Tbs. **Jerk Seasoning** ☀
1 tsp. **Seasoned Sea Salt** ☀
1/4 – 1/2 c. chopped onions

*Double recipe for 8 servings

- Mix meat, seasonings and onions well.
- Make into 4 patties.**
- Slightly oil (or use non-stick) frying pan.
- Cook turkey over medium heat for 5 – 7 minutes each side. Turkey should be well done but juicy. Cook beef to desired doneness.
- Can also be grilled.

Lo-cal, lo-fat appetizer idea: Form **Jerk Burger mix into 1 inch balls. Spray teflon pan with food spray and cook balls over low heat until brown and cooked through, (only takes a few minutes), shaking pan frequently. Keep warm in chafing dish and serve **Spicee Catsup** ☀ and **Tangy Tropical Ting** ☀ as dipping sauces.

Sweet Potato "Ting"

6 sweet potatoes* (about 2 lbs.)
Olive oil or unsalted butter
BBQ Seasoning ☀ to taste –
   depending on desired "saltiness"

* important to have good, firm,
   unblemished potatoes

- Peel potatoes, cutting off small pointed ends.
- Cut each potato into quarters (or, if very large, cut crosswise into halves and then quarter halves (finger food size!).
- Hold potatoes in large bowl of water, with about 1 tbs. cider vinegar and dash of salt.
- When ready to cook: oil 3 – 4 large sheets of heavy foil.
- Drain and dry potatoes pieces in dish towel and toss in bowl with enough oil to coat.
- Divide pieces amongst sheets of foil.
- Sprinkle with **BBQ Seasoning** ☀.
- Fold up foil loosely to cover and seal well.
- Cook on grill for about 15 – 20 minutes depending on heat and size of potatoes.
- Unwrap, sprinkle with more **BBQ Seasoning** ☀ if desired.

Rasta Pasta

One of my favourite recipes remained nameless for a vexing amount of time. But one day, as I was was serving this salad to guests, the obvious came to me in a flash ! This spicy, colourful, vegetarian dish, embodying Rastafarian red, gold and green with "Dreads" shaped pasta, truly conjures up the Island "Irie" spirit.

12 oz. pasta: tomato, pepper or
  "spicy" flavoured* (Fusilli is best)
2 Tbs. salad oil
2 cloves garlic, minced
4 lg scallion whites, sliced
2-1/2 c. green, red and yellow
  peppers cut into half inch dice
1 tsp. beef bouillon powder or 1 cube
  dissolved in 2/3 c. hot water
1/4 c. finely chopped red onion
1 Tbs. **Super Spice** ☀
1 tsp. **BBQ Seasoning** ☀
2 tsp. **Hot Pepper Vinegar** ☀
1/4 c. scallion greens, sliced
Caribbee Hot Sauce ☀ to taste

- Cook pasta "al dente".
- Drain and cool.
- Saute garlic and scallions in oil over medium heat about 3 min. (do not brown).
- Add peppers and bouillon mix.
- Cook slowly for 5 minutes.
- Cool and add chopped red onions, seasonings and vinegar.
- Add mixture to cooled pasta.
- Add scallion greens and adjust seasoning.
- Add more oil if necessary (or 1 – 2 Tbs. mayonnaise).

Serves 8 – 10

* If using plain pasta adjust seasonings to taste and add dash of
  Caribbee Hot Sauce ☀ if you want more heat

Mauby

Mauby is a spirited island designed drink, which is a delicious, digestive accompaniment to this highly seasoned cookout.

For each drink:
2 – 3 Tbs. **Mauby** Syrup
10 – 12 oz. club soda

- In a tall glass mix **Mauby**  with club soda.
- Add ice and garnish with lemon slice.

Ginger Surprise

The surprise is how easy and good these are !

1 recipe **Ginger Snaps** (p. 85)
cream cheese
Mango or Papaya **Chutney**

- Spread cream cheese on ginger snaps.
- Top each with a dollop of **Chutney** and a second "Snap".

Tea Time Teasers

Time Out Tournament Tea

Our friends are invited for an after-noon of challenging sport…be it golf, tennis, croquet, badminton or polo. The competition is keen and we all deserve a break to revive and refresh and to review our game.

Spiced Melon Balls

Presto Pesto Mini Pizza

Ginger Snaps

Pimms Polo Punch

Spiced Melon Balls

1 honeydew melon (make into balls)
1 cantaloupe melon (make into balls)
1/2 c. water
1/2 c. **Sugar 'N' Spice** ☀
1/2 tsp. **Vanilla-Vanilla** ☀
  or to taste
1/4 c. port wine or marsala
1/4 c. **Papaya** or **Mango Chutney** ☀

- Put melon balls into bowl. Chill.
- In a saucepan, heat water, **Sugar 'N' Spice** ☀, **Vanilla-Vanilla** ☀, wine, and **Chutney** ☀ until sugar melts and mixtures is smooth. Cool.
- Add mixture to fruit. Marinate refrigerated for at least 3 hours.
- Serve with toothpicks.

Presto Pesto Mini Pizza

Presto-Pesto Sauce III*
One package (tube) "All Ready" Pizza Crust
2 medium size tomatoes, chopped
2 – 3 sliced scallions
1/2 c. grated parmesan cheese
1 c. grated mozzarella

- Prepare **Presto Pesto Sauce III.***
- Prepare dough for pizza according to package directions.
- Spread layer of pesto sauce over dough.
- Top with tomatoes and scallions
- Sprinkle cheeses over all.
- Bake according to package directions.
- Cut into bite-size pieces with pizza cutter.

*Presto Pesto Sauce III
6 – 6-1/2 Tbs. **Presto Pesto** ☀
6 Tbs. parmesan cheese
6 Tbs. olive oil

- Heat all ingredients over moderate heat for 1-2 minutes (do not boil!)
- Let cool to room temp. before using.

Ginger Snaps

1 stick unsalted butter
1/2 cup white sugar
1/2 c. **Sugar 'N' Spice** ☀
1/2 c. dark molasses
2 c. flour
1 tsp. baking soda
1-1/2 tsp. **Ginger**
1/4 c. finely chopped Crystallized
   Ginger Gems ☀
1 egg beaten

- Preheat oven to 350°.
- Cream butter and sugars.
- Add molasses and mix well.
- Mix in dry ingredients, blending well.
- Fold **Ginger Gems** ☀ into mixture.
- Add egg and blend until smooth.
- Drop dough by teaspoons on greased cookie sheet.
- Bake 10-15 minutes.

Pimms Polo Punch

1/4 c. **Caribbee Spiced Tea** ☀
1 c. hot water
3 c. club soda
1 c. Pimms No. I Cup
6 orange slices
6 lemon slices
6 cucumber slices
sprigs of mint

- In a pitcher dissolve **Caribbee Spiced Tea** ☀ in hot water.
- When completely dissolved add club soda and Pimms.*
- Pour punch over ice in 6 tall glasses or goblets.
- Put slices of orange, lemon and cucumber in each glass.
- Garnish with sprigs of mint.

Serves 6

*Add approximately 6 oz. gin or vodka for a real crowd pleaser

Beagle Tea

A "proper tea" after an invigorating
day in the countryside … silver tea
service, our best china and an array
of refreshments for every taste …
the highlight of a convivial
sporting day.

Teriyaki Cocktail Biscuits
Pickled Shrimp
Tortellini with Pesto Cream
Pineapple Bacon Bites
Papaya Jam Bars
Tea Sandwiches
Martinique Cup

Teriyaki Cocktail Biscuits

Teriyaki Steak (p. 147)
Herbal Biscuits (p. 140)
Hearty Hors D'oeuvre Spread*

*Hearty Hors D'oeuvre Spread:
8 oz. cream cheese
1/4 c. unsalted butter
1/4 c. sour cream
2 cloves garlic, crushed
1/2 tsp. ground **Spiced
  Peppercorns** ☀
1 Tbs. and 1 tsp. **Mixed Hearty
  Herbs** ☀ crushed or ground in
  spice grinder
pinch **Seasoned Sea Salt** ☀
  to taste

• Thinly slice steak.
• Double or triple basic biscuit
  recipe, but substitute **Mixed
  Hearty Herbs** ☀ for **Presto
  Pesto** ☀

STEP I: Make Spread
• Beat cheese and butter until
  light.
• Add remaining ingredients and
  mix well.
• Chill several hours or preferably
  overnight.
• Serve (or spread)at room temp.

STEP II: Assemble Biscuits
• Split biscuits and spread each
  side with thin covering of softened **Hearty Hors D'oeuvre
  Spread**.
• Place thin slices of steak on
  biscuit half and cover with other
  half or serve "open faced".

Pickled Shrimp

2 lbs. medium shrimp cleaned and deveined
1/2 c. celery tops
1 **Bay Leaf**
Few **Spiced Peppercorns** ☀
parsley sprigs
1 c. sliced scallions
1/4 c. capers
2 tsp. **Celery Seed**
Marinade*
Chopped parsley

Marinade:*
1-1/4 c. salad oil
3/4 c. **Lime Vinegar** ☀
2 – 3 cloves garlic minced
2 tsp. **Mild Savory Herbs** ☀
1 tsp. **Island Fish Spice** ☀
3 Tbs. parmesan cheese
2 oz. can anchovies - mashed with its oil
- Place all in covered jar and shake vigorously until well blended.

- In pan cover shrimp and celery tops **Bay Leaf, Spiced Peppercorns** ☀ and parsley with boiling water.
- Simmer until just barely done (3 – 5 min.)
- Rinse with cold water to stop cooking, drain and pat dry.
- In large bowl mix scallions, capers and celery seed with shrimp.

- Make **Marinade** and pour into bowl of shrimp (or use ziplock bag).
- Cover and chill for 24 hours, spooning **Marinade** over occasionally.
- Drain excess liquid and serve shrimp on platter.
- Garnish with chopped parsley.

****This marinade makes an excellent **Ceasar Salad** dressing.

Tortellini with Pesto Cream

STEP I:

Pesto Cream Sauce

1/4 c. butter

1-1/2 c. heavy cream

2-1/2 – 3 Tbs. **Presto Pesto** ☀

freshly ground **Nutmeg**

dash of **Cayenne Pepper**

Seasoned Sea Salt ☀

* chopped parsley and/or basil for
  added colour and flavour can also
  be whisked in

STEP II: **Tortellini**

1 large package cheese tortellini

STEP III: **Service**

Bamboo skewers

water cress

parsley

fresh basil sprigs

STEP I:

- Simmer butter and cream until
  slightly thickened.
- Whisk in **Presto Pesto** ☀ and
  remaining seasonings.
- Continue simmering, stirring
  constantly for a few minutes.
- Add **Seasoned Sea Salt** ☀ to
  taste, if needed.*
- For dipping sauce: chill until
  serving time (sauce will thicken)
  but *serve at room temperature*.

STEP II:

- Bring a large pot of salted water
  to a boil and cook tortellini until
  just tender. Drain.

STEP III:

- Put 2 – 3 tortellini on each
  skewer.
- Put **Pesto Cream Sauce** in a
  bowl and place on a platter
  surrounded by tortellini skewers.
- Garnish platter with water cress,
  parsley or fresh basil sprigs.

≈ For dinner pasta sauce: Immediately toss cooked pasta with **Pesto Cream Sauce** (thin with milk if necessary) and serve.

≈ A flavourful variation: Toss hot pasta with chopped fresh tomatoes and sliced cooked Italian sausage before adding sauce.

Pineapple Bacon Bites

1 medium size fresh pineapple
  (or 1 can (20 oz,) pineapple
  chunks drained.
1/4 c. **Mango** or **Papaya**
  Chutney ☀
1/4 tsp. **Cinnamon**
1/8 tsp. ground **Cayenne Pepper**
12 slices bacon*

*Partially cook bacon before cut-
  ting and wrapping, so that it will
  crisp and brown evenly when
  skewered and broiled

- Remove top from pineapple and slice pineapple lengthwise into quarters. Remove core from each quarter.
- Cut fruit in one piece from rind and cut each quarter crosswise into 1 inch pieces.
- Mix together **Chutney** ☀, **Cinnamon** and **Cayenne Pepper** in large bowl.
- Add pineapple, and mix well.
- Cut bacon, cross wise into thirds.
- Wrap each pineapple slice with bacon and secure with toothpick.
- Preheat broiler and broil "bites" 5 – 7 min. or until bacon is crisp.

Papaya Jam Bars

1/2 c. butter
1/4 c. white sugar
1/4 c. **Sugar 'N' Spice** ☀
1/2 tsp. **Vanilla-Vanilla** ☀
1/2 tsp. almond flavouring
1 egg
1-1/2 c. flour
1 tsp. baking powder
1/2 tsp. salt
1/2 c. **Papaya Jam** ☀

- Preheat over to 400°
- Cream together butter, sugars, **Vanilla-Vanilla** ☀ and almond extracts.
- Stir in egg and blend well.
- In another bowl, sift together dry ingredients. Add to butter mixture and blend well.
- Butter an 8-inch square baking dish and spread with half the mixture. Cover with a layer of **Papaya Jam** ☀. Spread the rest of the dough on top.
- Bake 25 min.
- Cool. Cut into bars.

Tea Sandwiches

I. Radish and Sprout Sandwiches

Sunny Caribbee Boursin (p. 96)
Thinly sliced bread*
Thin slices of radish
sprouts

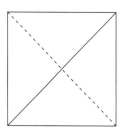

- Prepare **Sunny Caribbee Boursin.**
- Remove crusts from bread.
- Lightly spread each slice with softened **Boursin,** covering to edge.
- Top each bread slice with sliced radishes.
- Put sprouts on top of radishes and top all with another slice of bread.
- Cut each into 2 triangles (or into quarters depending on size of bread).**

II. Cucumber Dill

Dill Mayonnaise:
1-1/2 Tbs. **Down Island Dill** ☀
1 c. mayonnaise
Seasoned Sea Salt ☀, to taste
Thinly sliced bread*
paper thin slices of peeled
   cucumbers

- Combine **Down Island Dill** ☀, **Seasoned Sea Salt** ☀ and mayonnaise. Let mellow.
- For variety, cut bread into 2-inch rounds with cookie cutter.
- Spread each round to edge with a light layer of mayonnaise.
- Cover each round with slices of cucumber then top with another.**

*Thinly sliced light rye or whole wheat bread is a good change from white bread or use a combination.

**Sandwiches should be wrapped well in foil, plastic wrap or dampened cloths until ready to serve.

〰 Serve on a tray garnished with watercress or parsley, radish roses and sprouts.

Martinique Cup

1 qt. water
1/4 c. **California Coffee Mix**
  (p. 24)
6 oz. rum
Cinnamon Stick
whipped cream
Nutmeg or **Spice Island Cocoa
  Ball** ☀

- In heat proof pitcher combine boiling water and **Coffee Mix.**
- Stir until crystals dissolve.
- Add rum and mix.
- Pour into mugs or heat proof glasses.
- Stir with **Cinnamon Stick** and add dollop whipped cream sprinkled with grated **Nutmeg** or **Spice Island Cocoa Ball** ☀

This is a "Big Time" Tea. A lot of things can be done ahead, or give a few
  friends some recipes to make.

Make ahead and freeze:
- **Herbal Biscuits** (p. 140)

2 days before:
- Make **Hearty Hors D'oeuvre Spread**
- Bake **Papaya Jam Bars**
- Make **Pesto Cream Sauce**
- Marinate Shrimp

1 day before:
- Cook **Teriyaki Steak** (p. 147)
- Prepare Tea Sandwiches
- Partially cook bacon and prepare **Pineapple Bacon Bites**

Morning of the Tea:
- Have **Martinique Cup** ingredients ready.
- Thaw **Herbal Biscuits** and prepare with **Hearty Hors D'oeuvre Spread**– rewrap and return to fridge.
- Thinly slice steak, wrap and return to fridge.

Hour before Tea Time:
- Assemble steak sandwiches (or serve biscuits and meat separately with bowl of **Hearty Hors D'oeuvre Spread**).
- Cook tortellini and put on skewers.

Tea Time:
- Broil **Pineapple Bacon Bites**
- Assemble all else on suitable, serving dishes - garnish.
- Make tea and **Martinique Cup.**

Voila! Beagle Tea.

Mountain Magic and Trailside Treats

Enjoy the glories of

nature in the great outdoors ...

fresh air and sunshine, majestic

scenery and the peace and quiet of a

secret and special world.

Ham Roll-Ups

Mango Nut Bread with Honey Butter

Coconut Drops

Mulled Wine

Tropical Frappé

Ham Roll-Ups (For Hungry Hikers)

Celebrated "Boursin" is best known as a piquant hors d'oeuvre spread but it also contributes great character to a variety of recipes.

8 oz. pack thinly sliced boiled ham

Sunny Caribbee Boursin:
8 oz. cream cheese
4 oz. unsalted butter
3 – 4 tsp. **Herb Pepper** ☀

• Blend softened cheese and butter. Add **Herb Pepper** ☀ and mix well. Let mellow in refrigerator for several hours (the longer the better).

• Spread each ham slice with softened **Boursin**.

• Roll, lengthwise, sealing finished edge with extra **Boursin** if necessary.

• Wrap tightly in plastic wrap and chill until **Boursin** is firm.

• Slice into 1 inch pieces.**

** If taking on picnic, hike or whatever, wrap in heavy duty foil packs to keep cool and to hold shape.

≈ When using Boursin for an hors d'oeuvre spread, bring to room temperature before serving.

Mango Nut Bread

1-3/4 c. flour
2 tsp. baking powder
1/4 tsp. baking soda
1/2 tsp. salt
1/3 c. butter or shortening
1/3 c. sugar
1/3 c. **Sugar 'N' Spice** ☀
2 eggs
1 c. ripe mango, mashed
1/2 c. chopped nuts (optional)

• Preheat oven to 350°.

• Sift together flour, baking powder, soda and salt.

• Cream the butter with sugars.

• Add eggs and beat until fluffy.

• Blend the dry ingredients into the butter mixture, then mix in mangos.

• Pour into greased loaf pan.

• Bake 1 hour or until springy to touch and toothpick comes out clean.

Honey Butter

1 c. butter softened
1/3 c. **West Indian Honey** ☀
2 Tbs. orange juice concentrate

• Combine butter, **W.I. Honey** ☀ and orange juice concentrate in food processor or blender until smooth.

Coconut Drops

2 (3-1/2 oz.) cans Baker's South-
   ern-style coconut
1/2 c. **Sugar 'N' Spice** ☀
1/2 c. light brown sugar
1/2 c. flour
1/2 tsp. salt
1/4 c. butter
4 egg yolks
1/2 tsp. **Vanilla-Vanilla** ☀
Optional: grated rind of 1/2 lime

- Preheat oven to 350°.
- Place all ingredients in a bowl and mix thoroughly.
- Form the mix into 1-inch coconut balls.
- Place 2 inches apart on greased cookie sheet.
- Bake 20-30 minutes or until golden.

Mulled Wine

1/3 c. **Sugar 'N' Spice** ☀
3 Tbs. sugar
1/3 c. water
4 **Cloves**
2 **Cinnamon Sticks**
3 Tbs. **Ginger Beer Syrup** ☀
several pieces lemon and
   orange peel
1 bottle red wine, port or cider

- Place **sugars**, water, spices, **Ginger Beer Syrup** ☀ and peels in pan.
- Simmer, stirring often for 15 min.
- Strain syrup and add wine.
- Reheat just to simmer
- Pour into mugs* and garnish with lemon or orange slice.

* for picnic or hike, put in thermos.

Serves 6

Tropical Frappé

For each serving:
1 c. orange juice
1 banana cut into chunks
4 – 5 fresh strawberries, hulled.
1 – 2 Tbs. **West Indian Honey** ☀
1 tsp. **Sorrel Syrup** ☀

- Place all ingredients in blender or food processor along with 1 cup of crushed ice.
- Blend until smooth.
- Pour into tall glass (or thermos).
- Garnish with lime slice or whole strawberry.

〰 Your choice of hot or cold drink will be determined by locale and time of year.

Sundowners

Twilight Tapas

Pepper Crusted Salmon • Sausage Balls • Mushrooms Boursin • Calypso Chicken Skewers with Pineapple and Peppers • Tabouleh Stuffed Tomatoes

Sunset Sizzlers

Spiced Beef Curried Puffs • Olives Niçoise • Herbal Chèvre Log • Red Sails in the Sunset Rum Tea

Sip & Dip

Avocado Salsa with Tortilla Chips • "Hot" Artichoke Crab Gratin • Tzatziki with Pita Crisps • Sea Sick Sippers

Twilight Tapas

A pre concert or theatre party...

"Hearty Hors D'oeuvres;"

substantial sustenance to carry you

through the evening until the little

supper after the show.

(For some, this *is* supper!)

Pepper Crusted Salmon

Sausage Balls

Mushrooms Boursin

Tabouleh Stuffed Tomatoes

Calypso Chicken Skewers

Pepper Crusted Salmon

I. Marinade
> 2 Tbs. **B-2 Sauce** ☀
> 1 lg. clove garlic crushed
> 2 tsp. lemon juice

II. Salmon
> 1 – 1-1/4 lb. center cut salmon, filet*, skinned
> 4 tsp. **Herb Pepper** ☀
> 2 Tbs. lite olive oil

* 1 – 1-1/4 lb. salmon serves 2-3 for main course. For appetizer or Hors D'oeuvres you will need to cook several filets.

- Combine all ingredients for marinade in a large ziplock bag.
- Place salmon in marinade bag and marinate in fridge (turning bag several time to coat evenly).
- After 1/2 hr., remove salmon from bag and pat dry.
- Press pepper into filet, coating thoroughly.
- Heat oil in skillet over moderate-high heat.(Do not let smoke)
- Sauté for about 2 – 3 minutes on each side (depending on the thickness) until it flakes.
- When done, drain, blot on paper towels.
- Do not overcook! inside should be somewhat transparent when you remove from heat as it will continue to cook

Serving Suggestions:
1. **Buffet Hors D'oeuvres:** cook salmon ahead of time. Serve chilled on platter garnished with lemon wedges, watercress or parsley. For a large group of people: place 2 filets on platter, in shape of fish, filling space between filets with sprigs of parsley or watercress. Serve with thinly sliced cocktail breads.
2. **Individual Hor D'oeuvres:** cook salmon ahead of time. Chill. Just before serving, make individual Hors D'oeuvres. Place chunk of salmon on Melba toast, water biscuits or cocktail bread. Squeeze a bit of lemon juice on salmon. Garnish with capers and finely minced red onion.
3. **First or appetizer course:** serve hot or cold small portions with mixed greens, capers, scallion slices and lemon garnish.
4. **Main course:** serve hot.

Sausage Balls

1 lb. mild sausage (bulk)
1 tsp. **Mild Savory Herbs** ☀
1 slightly beaten egg
6 Tbs. bread crumbs
1/2 c. **Spicee Catsup** ☀
3 Tbs. **Sugar 'N' Spice** ☀
1-1/2 Tbs. white wine
1-1/2 Tbs. soy sauce

• Mix sausage, **Mild Savory Herbs** ☀, egg, and crumbs thoroughly and roll into small 1 inch balls.
• Using teflon skillet, lightly coated with food spray, brown slowly on all sides.
• Combine **Spicee Catsup** ☀, **Sugar 'N' Spice** ☀, wine, and soy sauce and pour over balls.
• Cover and simmer 30 minutes.
• Transfer to chafing dish.
Yields about 3 – 4 dozen balls.

As a zesty condiment or as a recipe ingredient, sugar-free **Spicee Catsup** ☀ imparts more flavour without extra calories

Mushrooms Boursin

3 to 4 doz. bite-sized mushrooms
Sunny Caribbee Boursin Cheese
(p. 96)

• Preheat oven to 350°
• Clean mushrooms and remove stems.
• Fill mushrooms with cheese and arrange on cookie sheet.
• Bake 20 min.
• Sprinkle with chopped parsley or chives for colour and serve on a decorative platter.

Calypso Chicken Skewers

1-1/2 lbs. boneless, skinless chicken
  breast
1 tbs. balsamic vinegar
1/3 c. red wine
1/2 c. **Sunny Caribbee Chutney** ☀
1/4 c. olive oil
2 – 3 peppers (green, red and
  yellow) cut into 1 inch squares
1 can pineapple chunks, drained or
  fresh pineapple cut into small
  squares

- Cut chicken into small cubes and put into large bowl (or ziplock bag).
- Add vinegar, wine, **Chutney** ☀ and olive oil to chicken. marinate 4 hours or overnight.
- Drain chicken. Put on bamboo skewers alternating with peppers and pineapple.
- Grill, turning over hot coals for 8 to 10 min.

Healthy Hints for Hors D'oeuvres

Escape the ubiquitous chip, dipper, cracker, bread syndrome.
Treat everybody to healthy, low fat, low salt, low calorie,
crisp and crunchy substitutes.

Cherry Tomatoes: Scooped out cherry tomatoes are delicious filled with any meat, fish, or egg salad or herbal cheese mixes as well as **Tabouleh** (p. 105)

Cucumber and Zucchini slices: Cut cucumber and zucchini into 1/4" slices and spread with **Boursin, Curry-Chutney Cheese** or your favourite spread.

Cucumber Boats: Peel cucumber and cut in halves. Cut a lengthwise strip from rounded side so "boats" will sit flat. Remove seeds and fill "boats" with any of the above: chicken salad, creamed cheese and salmon, or cottage cheese and chopped veggies. Cut into 1 inch pieces.

Celery: Peel strings from large celery sticks and proceed in same manner as for cucumber boats.

Snow Peas: Blanch snow peas for 30 seconds, drain, dry and pop one side open. Fill with any softened cream cheese mixture such as **Boursin** or **Hearty Hors D'oeuvre Spread**. Use fillings that will firm up when chilled and that won't turn soupy when served.

Belgian Endive: A great dipper or fill with mixtures suitable to snow peas.

Mushroom Caps: Raw or cooked, like cherry tomatoes can be successfully filled with most anything. Try finely minced ham or corned beef and **Chutney** ☀.

Tabouleh Stuffed Tomatoes

Tabouleh:

1 c. bulgur (cracked wheat)
1-1/4 c. hot water
2 Tbs. **Lemon Grass Vinegar** ☀
1/4 c. oil
1 c. finely chopped tomatoes
1/2 c. cucumber (peeled, seeded
   and finely chopped)
1/4 c. scallions, thinly sliced
2 – 3 cloves garlic minced
1/2 c. finely chopped parsley
1 Tbs. **Presto Pesto** ☀
1 tsp. **Mixed Hearty Herbs** ☀
Seasoned Sea Salt ☀ and **Herb**
   Pepper ☀ to taste
medium size cherry tomatoes

- In large bowl, pour hot water and **Lemon Grass Vinegar** ☀ over bulgur.
- Let sit until all liquid is absorbed (30 – 40 min.)
- Add oil and remaining ingredients.
- Toss, fluff and chill for several hours to blend flavors.
- Cut tomatoes in half.*
- Scoop out seeds and pulp with melon baller.
- Drain on paper towels.
- Stuff each half with **Tabouleh**.

* If tomatoes are small, cut thin slice off stem end, scoop out centers and
  stuff the whole tomato.

Alternative Serving Suggestions:

For "Alternatives", coarsely chopped vegetables are better.
Add chopped green and/or red pepper and crumbled feta cheese.
   1. Serve over bed of lettuce as a side salad.
   2. Stuff large tomato for a dinner or lunch "vegetable".
   3. Serve with pita bread for a veggie sandwich
   4. Substitute for potato, pasta or rice at any time.

Sunset Sizzlers

Summer, when it sizzles, calls for cool, simple, light refreshment while awaiting the ritual sunset and the magic of afterglow.

Curried Puffs with Spiced Beef

Olives Niçoise

Herbal Chèvre Log

Red Sails in the Sunset Rum Tea

Curried Puffs with Spiced Beef

STEP I:

6 oz. canned corned beef

1 tsp. **Island Nutmeg Mustard**
   (prepared)

2 tsp. **Papaya** or **Mango**
   Chutney

3 Tbs. sour cream

3 Tbs. mayonnaise

• Mix all ingredients.

STEP II: Hors D'oeuvre Puffs

1 tsp. **Caribbee Curry**

• Make basic puffs according to
   recipe (p. 32), but eliminate crab
   meat, **Mild Savory Herbs** and
   Fish Spice and substitute
   with 1 Tbs. **Caribbee Curry**.
   Proceed with same directions.

STEP III: Assemble Hor D'oeuvres

• Cut puffs in half.

• Fill puffs with corned beef mix
   just before serving.

Olives Niçoise

1 lb. brine cured olives (Italian,
   Greek or French)

3/4 c. extra virgin olive oil (don't
   use lite oil here)

1 Tbs. lemon juice

2 large garlic cloves, minced

1 Tbs. **Mixed Hearty Herbs**

1 tsp. crushed **Rosemary**

• Drain olives and pat dry.

• Combine all ingredients in a bowl.

• Cover bowl and marinate in
   refrigerator for several days,
   stirring occasionally.

• Let come to room temperature
   before serving.

〰 This makes a deliciously different holiday or hostess gift. Put into a
   pretty container (or a recycled **Sunny Caribbee** handmade jar) and tie
   with a perky ribbon.

Herbal Chèvre Log

1 log of Chèvre* (goat cheese)
your choice of herb blend:
> **Mixed Hearty Herbs** ☀,
> **Mild Savory Herbs** ☀,
> **Presto Pesto** ☀,
> **Spiced Peppercorns** ☀ or
> **Herb Pepper** ☀

- Sprinkle your choice of herb blend onto plate or piece of foil.
- Roll Chèvre log in herbs until totally covered.
- Press herbs into cheese
- Serve at room temperature with crackers or small breads.**

* can substitute cream cheese or farmer's cheese

** Use 1/4 inch slices of cucumber or zucchini as a low-cal and refreshing change. These crisp veggie slices also make a good base for prepared canapés. Just add your favorite topping.

Red Sails in the Sunset Rum Tea

1 qt. prepared **Caribbee Spiced Tea** ☀ (p. 24)
2 oz. or 4 Tbs. **Sorrel Syrup** ☀
1 c. white rum

- Combine all ingredients well and pour over ice in clear glasses.*
- Garnish with whole strawberry or fruit slices.

* Or serve an ambrosial hot drink in glass mugs.

Sip and Dip

Relax…soothe your body and soul.

Do nothing more than watch for the

"green flash".

Avocado Salsa with Tortilla Chips

"Hot" Artichoke Crab Gratin

Tzatziki with Pita Crisps

Sea-Sick Sippers

Avocado Salsa

1 c. prepared **Sunshine Salsa** (p. 76)

2 – 3 avocados, chopped and mashed

juice of 1/2 lemon

- Prepare **Salsa** (p. 76).
- To one cup of **Salsa** add avocados and lemon.
- Let sit several hours covered in fridge before serving .
- Before serving bring to room temperature.
- Serve with tortilla chips.

"Hot" Artichoke Crab Gratin

1 14 oz. can artichoke hearts, drained and coarsely chopped

2 c. mayonnaise (lite)

1 Tsp. **Super Spice** ☀

2 c. grated parmesan cheese

1-1/2 cups crab meat (fresh or canned) drained

1/2 – 1 tsp. **Caribbee Hot Sauce** ☀

- Preheat oven to 350°.
- Combine all ingredients, mix well. Spoon into shallow baking dish. (preferably a decorative one).
- Bake 15 – 20 min.
- Serve with crackers.

Tzatziki with Pita Crisps

Tzatziki (p. 124)
Four 7 inch pita bread
extra virgin olive oil
Seasoned Sea Salt ☀

- Preheat oven to 375°.
- Prepare **Tzatziki**.
- Split pitas.
- Brush rough side with olive oil and sprinkle lightly with **Seasoned Sea Salt** ☀.
- Cut into 8 pie-shaped wedges and place on baking sheet.
- Bake for 8 – 12 min. or until crisp and golden brown.
- Put **Tzatziki** into colourful bowl, place on platter and surround with pita chips.

≈ Pita crisps make tasty scoops, edible spoons and dippers for countless hors d'oeuvres.

≈ Belgian endive leaves also make good "dippers" for Tzatziki.

Sea Sick Sippers

The sure cure for motion sickness (**Ginger** and **Mauby** ☀ are the secret) but also a delicious, refreshing drink for the well.

For each serving:
2 Tbs. **Ginger Beer Syrup** ☀
4 – 6 oz. soda
1-1/2 oz. rum
freshly squeezed lemon or lime
 (about 1 tsp.)
a few dashes of **Mauby** ☀
mint sprigs

- In a large glass combine first four ingredients.
- Add ice and stir.
- Add a few dashes of **Mauby** ☀ (Caribbean Bitters) and sprigs of mint.

Divine Dinners

An Elegant Evening

A special dinner for special people.
A candlelit, flower adorned table set
with the best linens, china, silver and
crystal. There will be good conversation, good music, good food and
wine…a memorable evening.

Shrimp Côte D'Azur
Chutney Glazed Cornish Hens
Caribbee Curried Rice
Festival Vegetables
West Indian Flambé

Serves 6

Shrimp Côte D'Azur

6 Tbs. unsalted butter
2 – 3 cloves garlic crushed
6 – 8 scallions sliced (hold greens
    separately)
1/8 tsp. **Saffron**, crushed
2 lbs. large shrimp*
1 tsp. **Mild Savory Herbs** ☀
1/2 tsp. **Island Fish Spice** ☀
1/2 c. white wine or dry vermouth**

* scallops or lobster are good
    substitutes

**when white wine is called for,
    I always use dry vermouth, which
    has much more character. You
    will perhaps need less - so test
    with smaller amount

- Sauté garlic, scallion whites and
  Saffron until garlic and scallions
  are medium soft. Don't brown.
- Add raw, peeled and deveined
  shrimp and sauté until partially
  cooked.
- Can be made ahead to this point. ☾
- Add wine, seasonings and simmer
  until shrimp are done. Don't over
  cook shrimp.
- Test for salt and pepper.
- Sprinkle with sliced scallion
  greens and chopped parsley.

Serves 6 as appetizer

〰 For a great pasta sauce: add 1/2 c. olive oil, adjust seasonings, toss
    with 1 lb. pasta, sprinkle with greens

Mellow Yellow, a colloquial name for Saffron, is the world's most
precious "herb". It comes from the dried stigmas of *Crocus
Satvius*, a small purple flower grown primarily in Spain. The
flowers must be harvested during the short 15 – 20 day
flowering period and then the stigmas are laboriously removed
by hand. After being dried, the yield of approximately 160,000
flowers is a mere 1 kilogram (2-1/4 lbs.).
Saffron is valued for the brilliant colour and unique aromatic
taste that it brings to illustrious Italian Risotto and Cioppino,
French Bouillabaise, Spanish Paella and other Mediterranean
inspired culinary treasures.

Chutney Glazed Cornish Hens

6 Cornish hens
Seasoned Sea Salt ☀
Vegetable oil

Glaze:
3/4 c. **Mango** or **Papaya**
   Chutney ☀
3 Tbs. lemon juice or
   Lemon Grass Vinegar ☀
1-1/2 Tbs. **West Indian Honey** ☀
3 Tbs. butter
1 Tbs. **Caribbee Curry** ☀
1 Tbs. **B-2 Sauce** ☀

☾ Can be made ahead to this point.

- Preheat oven to 375°.
- Rinse and dry hens.
- Sprinkle interior with **Seasoned Sea Salt** ☀.
- Tie legs together. Bend wings under bird. Close cavities by covering with skin and securing with picks.
- Place in large baking pan and brush with oil. ☾
- Place hens in oven.

- Combine glaze ingredients in small pan and simmer for 10 minutes. ☾
- After hens have been in oven 20 minutes, brush each with glaze.
- Baste several times during remainder of cooking time which should be 20-40 minutes depending on weight of hens. Check temperature between thigh and body, with meat thermometer, Thermometer should read 180-185°.
  Skin should be brown and crispy.
- Remove from oven and let sit for 10 minutes before serving.

Additional **Chutney** ☀ is the appropriate condiment.

Caribbee Curried Rice

2 Tbs. butter
1 c. rice
2 – 3 Tbs. **Caribbee Curry** ☀
2-1/4 c. water

* 1 Tbs scallion whites, sliced or chopped shallots can be added and sauteed

** chopped chives or scallion greens and/or parsley are a colourful and tasteful addition

- Melt butter in medium saucepan.
- Add rice*.
- Sauté, stirring until translucent but not brown.
- Add **Caribbee Curry** ☀ and cook for about 1 minute.
- Add 2-1/4 c. water and bring to a boil over medium heat.
- Cover tightly, reduce heat, simmer until tender (about 20 minutes).
- Fluff with fork** and serve.

Festival Vegetables

Colourful, seasonal vegetables
Cut in "Julienne" sticks:
carrots, beets, summer squash, zucchini, parsnips, turnip. Your combination about 1/2 c. per person
Butter: enough to lightly coat cooked vegetables
Super Spice ☀

* **Mixed Hearty Herbs** ☀ or **Mild Savory Herbs** ☀ also work well or use an herbal butter made with approximately 1 Tbs. herb blend to 3/4 – 1 c. softened butter.

- Blanch each vegetable separately to crunchy stage.
- Drain and rinse well in cold water to stop cooking.
- Can be made ahead to this point. ☾
- 5 – 10 minutes before serving, melt butter in sauté pan.
- Heat vegetables just until hot enough to serve.
- Sprinkle with **Super Spice** ☀* to taste.
- Toss lightly and serve.

When real butter is indispensible to a recipe, I prefer to use the "unsalted" variety which allows the rich fresh flavour of pure butter to predominate. Without built-in salt, I can season to my taste.

West Indian Flambé

6 bananas, split lengthwise
1/3 c. butter, melted
1/3 c. **Sugar 'N' Spice** ☀
2 Tbs. lime juice
1/3 c. light or dark rum
Nutmeg

- Preheat oven to 350°.
- Place bananas in shallow buttered baking dish.
- Mix butter, **Sugar 'N' Spice** ☀ and lime juice.
- Pour over bananas.
- Bake for 20 minutes.
- In small pan, heat rum.
- Ignite and pour over bananas.
- When flame dies, serve bananas over ice cream or with dollop of whipped cream garnished with freshly grated **Nutmeg**.

This is an elegant but easily prepared dinner which allows you to spend more time with guests than in the kitchen.

Day Before:

Make glaze for cornish hens

Julienne and blanche vegetables

Morning of party:

1. Slice scallions for rice and shrimp

2. Prepare first two steps of shrimp recipe

3. Truss hens

1 hour before serving time place hens in oven.

1/2 hour before dinner prepare bananas for baking.

Twenty minutes before serving main course start cooking rice. Quickly finish cooking shrimp and serve your appetizer.

While hens are resting finish cooking vegetables.

During dinner bake bananas.

Backyard Barbecue Bacchanal

Don't worry…Don't hurry…

No problem BBQ. Come as you are

and enjoy an evening of

camaraderie, "grillside".

Sausage Spree
Bob's Grilled Salmon
Tzatziki
Riviera Potatoes
Pesto Onions
Sliced Tomatoes with Feta
Strawberries "Blue Strawbery"

Serves 4 – 6

Sausage Spree

Variety of sausages:
  Italian
  Chorizio
  Bratwurst
  Kielbasa
  Knockwurst
  Linguiça

Prepared **Island Nutmeg Mustard** ☀ (dilute with hot water if too thick for dipping)

- Prick skins of sausages in several places to release fat.
- Cook, covered on medium hot grill (turning frequently) until crispy on outside but still juicy inside. This should take about 8-10 minutes depending on thickness of sausage (should not be pink).
- Cut into 1 inch pieces. Serve with picks and **Nutmeg Mustard** ☀ as dipping sauce.

Tzatziki

2 lbs. small-medium cucumbers (about 6)
1 pt. sour cream or yogurt (lite)
1/2 Tbs. olive oil
1/2 Tbs. lemon juice
1-1/2 tsp. minced garlic
1-1/2 – 2 Tbs. **Down Island Dill** ☀
Seasoned Sea Salt ☀ to taste

- Peel, seed, and cut cucumbers into fine dice.
- Place in a dish towel and squeeze out excess moisture.
- Combine with remaining ingredients.
- Chill well (at least 2 hours to blend flavours).
- Serve with **Bob's Grilled Salmon**.

This makes an excellent sauce, dip or salad. Thinned with milk or cream, it makes a "Quickee Cucumber Soup" – adjust seasonings

Bob's Grilled Salmon

2 – 3 lbs. fresh salmon filet*
　1 – 1-1/4 inch thick
fresh lemon or lime juice
Island Fish Spice ☀
Olive oil (lite)

* Wire grill basket is necessary to easily and efficiently turn large filet

- Lay filet on platter, skin side down.
- Sprinkle juice lightly over flesh.
- Liberally sprinkle **Island Fish Spice** ☀ over all to make a light coating.
- Lightly brush with "lite" olive oil and let stand at room temperature 30 minutes.
- Heat grill to maximum temperature with cover down.
- Place filet in large grill basket* and cook for 5 minutes with flesh side down (uncovered).
- Turn and cook for 8-10 minutes with skin side down and grill cover closed (check frequently for flames caused by skin burning).
- Remove while inside of filet is very moist and still a bit translucent (don't over cook).
- Open wire basket and remove to platter with large metal spatula. Miraculously, the skin remains attached to grill basket as you remove the filet.
- Serve with **Tzatziki** (p.124) as accompanying sauce.

The purpose of a fish marinade is to flavour and to seal in moisture. Whereas marinades tenderize meat, fish will toughen if marinated for more than 30 minutes.

Riviera Potatoes

10 – 12 medium red bliss or white
  baking potatoes (about 2 lbs.)
3 Tbs. unsalted butter, melted
3 Tbs. lite olive oil
1 tsp. **Mixed Hearty Herbs** ☀
1/2 tsp. crushed Rosemary leaves
1 tsp. **Seasoned Sea Salt** ☀
1 tsp. **Herb Pepper** ☀
1 lg. clove garlic, minced

* Can cut potatoes in 1/2 inch dice
  and cook for less time

- Preheat oven to 450°.
- Leaving potatoes unpeeled, scrub
  and quarter.*
- Mix butter, oil, seasonings and
  garlic in large bowl.
- Add quartered potatoes and
  gently toss to coat each piece.
- Place coated potatoes skin side
  down in large shallow roasting
  pan .
- Roast in oven for 25 – 30 minutes (depending on size) or until
  brown, crispy and your desired
  "doneness".

To release maximum flavour and aroma from dried herbs, use an
herb grinder or crush herbs between fingers.

Pesto Onions

per person:
1 medium onion
1 tsp. butter
1 heaping tsp. **Presto Pesto** ☀

* Several quartered onions can be
  placed in larger packet of foil and
  cooked together

- Quarter onion.
- Place on large square of foil.
- Put butter and **Presto Pesto** ☀
  on top of onion.
- Securely but loosely seal foil
  around onion.*
- Cook on grill 20 – 30 minutes.

This is David's version of "**Greg's Curried Onions** (p.187) " which substitutes
Presto Pesto ☀ for **Caribbee Curry** ☀ or Jeanne suggests **Steak Spice** ☀

Sliced Tomatoes with Feta

Red ripe tomatoes
Hot Pepper Vinegar ☼
Seasoned Sea Salt ☼
Herb Pepper ☼
Presto Pesto ☼
Feta or Chèvre Cheese

- Cut tomatoes into 1/2 inch slices.
- Arrange pinwheel style on a round platter.
- Sprinkle lightly with **Hot Pepper Vinegar** ☼.
- Sprinkle with seasonings.
- Crumble feta or chèvre cheese over all.
- Chopped fresh chives and/or minced parsley sprinkled over all adds colour and flavour.

Strawberries "Blue Strawbery"

This is my adaptation of a brilliant, uncomplicated dessert, first experienced many years ago at the Blue Strawbery restaurant in Portsmouth, New Hampshire. It is a simple and refreshing finale to a large, rich dinner. My thanks to James Haller wherever he may now be.

per person:
about 6 large perfect strawberries* with stems left on
sour cream or yogurt (lite)
Sugar 'N' Spice ☼

* also works well with green grapes, fresh pineapple, peaches, etc.

- On individual plates arrange strawberries in a circle.
- Place a generous dollop of sour cream (or yogurt) on 1/2 of center of plate.
- Place generous Tbs. of **Sugar 'N' Spice** ☼ also in center.
- Dip strawberry first into sour cream and then into the sugar.

Midsummer Madness

Fun, frivolity and fantasy.

Celebrate the rites of summer with

fireworks and festive fare.

Plantation Punch

Greg's Jambalaya Louisiane

Pasta Con Vongole

Hearts of Lettuce, Virgin Island Style

Chèvre Crouton

Great Grapes

Serves 8

Plantation Punch

1 qt. strong prepared **Passion Fruit Tea** ☀ (see p. 53)
1 bottle white wine
1/2 c. **Guavaberry Liqueur** ☀

- Mix all and chill.
- Serve over ice and garnish with pineapple spears.

Greg's Jambalaya Louisiane

Greg, born in Rapides Parish, Louisiana, showed an affinity for Cajun cooking at an early age. This early influence inspired him, in later years, to create this nostalgic version of the Creole Classic.

1 lb. smoked or Italian sausage and/or ham
1/2 c. vegetable oil
2 medium onions, chopped (1/2 inch pieces)
1/2 c. celery, sliced (1/2 in. pieces)
1 large green pepper, chopped (1/2 inch pieces)
6 whole scallions, sliced into 1/4 inch pieces (set greens aside)
4 – 6 cloves garlic, minced
2 lbs. canned tomatoes (incl. juice)
1 can tomato paste (6 oz.)
1/2 lemon, quartered
1 tsp. **Mixed Hearty Herbs** ☀
1 tsp. **Island Fish Spice** ☀
2 lbs. raw shrimp (peeled and deveined)
Caribbee Hot Sauce ☀
Seasoned Sea Salt ☀
Spiced Peppercorns ☀
3 c. cooked rice

- Cut sausage into 1 inch slices.
- Cut ham into 1/2 inch cubes.
- Sauté in medium hot oil until lightly browned.
- Add next 5 ingredients.
- Lower heat and cook 5 minutes (do not brown).
- Add tomatoes with liquid, tomato paste, lemon and seasonings.
- Simmer for 10 minutes.
- Add raw, peeled shrimp and simmer until shrimp are pink and just opaque (do not over cook).
- Add **Caribbee Hot Sauce** ☀, **Seasoned Sea Salt** ☀ and **Spiced Peppercorns** ☀ to taste. (
- Add scallions and serve over rice in large individual shallow bowls or, if you prefer, combine all before serving.

(This may be made ahead to here (tastes better the next day !) but remove shrimp while reheating...and add only at last minute so as not to over cook and toughen.

An all age, crowd pleasing, main course option fits perfectly into this menu:

Pasta Con Vongole (Clam Sauce)

To Mark, Carol and family, whose appreciation of this recipe inspires me to make it over and over again.

1/3 c. olive oil

4 cloves garlic, minced

Two 6-1/4 oz. cans chopped clams

1/3 c. dry Vermouth

1-1/2 tsp. **Mild Savory Herbs** ☀

Seasoned Sea Salt ☀ and **Spiced Peppercorns** ☀ (ground) to taste

1/2 c. coarsely chopped fresh parsley

12 oz. pasta: linguine, fettucine, vermicelli, or angel hair

- Sauté garlic in oil until tender (do not brown).
- Add clam juice, vermouth, and **Mild Savory Herbs** ☀.
- Cook over low heat for 5 minutes and let sit.
- Cook linguine "al dente."
- Drain pasta and return to pot or warm serving bowl.
- Quickly reheat clam liquid.
- Add clams, **Seasoned Sea Salt** ☀ and **Spiced Peppercorns** ☀ to taste and heat for a minute or two.
- Combine sauce with warm pasta and quickly and lightly toss all with parsley before serving.

2 large servings, 3 average or 4 small

Hearts of Lettuce, Virgin Island Style

One year, we spent an "away from away" holiday at Sandy Ground, Jost Van Dyke. With no existing land transport, restaurants, stores or dependable electricity, our cooking and eating habits were necessarily very inventive. Our provisions consisted mainly of canned and "long-life" foods supplemented by the tiny commissary. Adapting our limited supplies, in as many ways as possible, **Virgin Island Dressing** proved to be a tasty sandwich spread, sauce for meat and fish, and a dressing for egg or tuna salad as well as "green".

Virgin Island Dressing:
1/2 c. Mayonnaise
1-1/2 Tbs**. Spicee Catsup** ☀
1 tsp. **Super Spice** ☀
1-1/2 Tbs. capers
2 Tbs. scallions, sliced

Iceberg lettuce*

- Combine salad dressing ingredients. Thin with small amount of lemon or caper juice if too thick.
- Core lettuce and cut into desired number and size wedges.
- Serve wedges on individual salad plates dressed with generous serving of **Virgin Island Dressing**.
- Garnish with parsley, chopped chives or radish slices.

*Iceberg lettuce, although not perhaps the most flavourful or interesting lettuce, is readily available and works well when simplicity is desired. This dressing also works well served over a plate of loose greens such as Bibb, Boston, Romaine lettuce or Belgian endive.

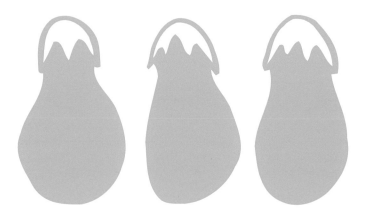

Chèvre Crouton

French Baguette
olive oil
1/2 lb. Chèvre cheese
Herb Pepper ☀

- Slice French Baguette into 1/4 inch thick pieces.
- Place slices on baking sheet and place under broiler until golden.
- Turn and brush other side lightly with oil.
- Evenly spread each slice with cheese, covering edges.
- Sprinkle with **Herb Pepper** ☀ to taste. ❨

❨ Can make ahead to here and broil at last minute or can totally make ahead and keep at room temperature

- Return pan to oven and broil only until cheese is slightly melted.

Great Grapes

2 lbs. large green seedless grapes cut into halves
1 c. sour cream
2 Tbs. **Sugar 'N' Spice** ☀
1/4 tsp. **Vanilla-Vanilla** ☀
freshly grated **Nutmeg**

- Mix grapes, sour cream, **Sugar 'N' Spice** ☀ and **Vanilla-Vanilla** ☀ in bowl.
- Chill for at least 2 hours.
- At serving time, spoon mixture into serving goblets or bowls.
- Sprinkle with a bit of **Sugar 'N' Spice** ☀, a bit of freshly grated **Nutmeg**, and sprigs of mint.

Less sugar is required in recipes using **Sugar 'N' Spice** ☀.
The addition of West Indian spices to natural brown sugar
yields a more complete and complex flavour than refined white
or ordinary brown sugar.

133

Bountiful Buffet

A gathering of the clan or visiting friends and dignitaries…a colourful array of dishes that can rise to any number or occasion…an easy to prepare crowd pleaser

Butterflied Leg of Lamb à la Bob
Barley Pilaf
Sunshine Salad
Honey-Ginger Glazed Carrots
Sesame Broccoli
Herbal Biscuit Ring
Dessert Coffee Californian

Serves 10-12

Butterflied Leg of Lamb à la Bob

6 – 7 lb. butterflied leg of lamb
Marinade:
1/4 c. olive oil (lite)
1/3 c. lemon juice or **Lemon Grass Vinegar** ☀ or red wine
1 Tbs. finely minced garlic
3 Tbs. **Steak Spice** ☀
1 tsp. **Mixed Hearty Herbs** ☀
1 tsp. **Seasoned Sea Salt** ☀
freshly ground **Spiced Peppercorns** ☀
2 tsp. dried **Rosemary** (crushed or put through herb grinder)
1/4 c. finely chopped parsley (or 3 – 4 tsp. dried)

- Combine all ingredients for marinade in shallow baking dish, large enough to hold lamb.
- Place lamb in dish and rub thoroughly with marinade.
- Cover dish with food wrap and refrigerate for at least 12 hours (turning once).
- Scrape off most of the marinade, reserving for basting.
- Bring meat to room temperature before grilling.
- Grill* about 5 inches from heat for about 10 minutes per side for medium-rare.**
- After removing from heat, let sit 5-10 minutes before slicing.

* Use wire grill basket to hold meat together and facilitate turning

**Use meat thermometer to check temperature at various points of thickness. Remove large cuts of meat from grill when temperature reads 5 degrees lower than suggested, allowing juices to set. Temperature will rise to desired "doneness" in 5-10 minutes sitting time.

Marinades flavour as well as tenderize meats. The oil moistens while the acidic ingredients (wine, vinegar, yogurt or citric juices) tenderize and flavour. The selected sesonings determine the real character of your marinade.
One to 3 hours at room temerature or overnight in the fridge is the optimum marinating time.

Barley Pilaf

2 c. barley
1 **Bouquet Garni** ☀
1/3 c. butter
1 large onion, chopped
1/2 lb. fresh mushrooms
1 Tbs. dry instant bouillon mix
1 tsp. **Mixed Hearty Herbs** ☀
1 tsp. **Seasoned Sea Salt** ☀
1/2 tsp. browning sauce: Gravy
  Master or Kitchen Bouquet
1/4 c. fresh parsley

Serves 10-12

- Cook barley with **Bouquet Garni** ☀ in large amount of water until just tender. Drain.
- Sauté onions and thickly sliced mushrooms in butter until tender.
- Add bouillon, seasonings, and browning sauce.
- Combine all with Barley. ☾
- Heat all slowly until heated thru.
- Mix in parsley just before serving.

☾ This may be made ahead and frozen in plastic container or ziplock bag. If planning to freeze, cook barley less time as it tends to soften more when frozen, and delete mushrooms. Add parsley and sauteéd mushrooms after defrosted and reheated.

Sunshine Salad

32 oz. can V-8 Juice
2 envelopes (2 Tbs.) unflavoured
  gelatin
2 Tbs. **Sunshine Salsa** ☀

* when partially thickened,
  chopped scallions, celery, pepper,
  etc., may be folded into mix.

Serves 6-8

- Dissolve gelatin in 1/2 c. cold V-8.
- Bring to a boil: 1 c. V-8 and 2 tbs. **Sunshine Salsa** ☀.
- Add the gelatin mix to the hot liquid, stirring well until gelatin is totally dissolved.
- Add remaining cold V-8 juice and mix well.
- Pour into quart size mold (sprayed with food spray) and chill well* until firm.
- Serve on a bed of lettuce. Garnish with cottage cheese, chopped chives, parsley and/or raw veggies pieces

Honey-Ginger Glazed Carrots

3 lbs. baby carrots* trimmed and peeled

2 Tbs. unsalted butter

3 Tbs. **West Indian Honey** ☀

2 Tbs. fresh orange or lemon juice

2 Tbs. finely chopped Crystallized **Ginger Gems** ☀

Seasoned Sea Salt ☀ to taste

1 tsp. grated lemon or orange peel

* If baby carrots are not available, cut large ones into 3-4 inch sections, then quarter sections

- Blanch carrots to crunchy stage.
- Melt butter in large sauté pan.
- Add **Honey** ☀, juice and **Ginger Gems** ☀.
- Combine well, stirring over medium heat until smooth.
- Add carrots and cook over medium heat until carrots are well glazed and heated through.
- Add dash **Seasoned Sea Salt** ☀ if desired.
- Serve with grated peel sprinkled over all.

12 large servings

The use of honey, having nearly twice the sweetening power of sugar, is a natural and healthy way to sweeten foods.
West Indian Honey ☀ is especially flavourful and unique because of the exotic and fragrant plants and flowers from which bees gather nectar. It is said that honey bees tap two million flowers to make one pound of honey.
Honey can be kept indefinately if stored in a cool, dry place; not in the refrigerator where it will crystallize. If crystallization does occur, reliquify by placing uncovered jar in the microwave oven or in a bowl of hot water.

Sesame Broccoli

This makes approximately 4-6 servings but can easily be made larger to serve any number. Double recipe for this menu.

1 bunch broccoli (1 lb.)

- Remove broccoli florets from stalks.
- Peel and slice the stalks into 1/4 inch slices or 1/2 inch dice.
- Blanch all in pot of boiling water for only about 1 minute — until still crunchy.

☾ can be prepared a day ahead

- Drain and chill. ☾

Sesame Dressing:
1-1/2 Tbs. sesame oil
1-1/2 Tbs. vegetable oil
1 – 2 cloves garlic, minced
1 Tbs. **Lemon Grass Vinegar** ☀
1 tsp. **Jerk Sauce** ☀
1 tsp. **Jerk Spice** ☀
1 tsp. **Seasoned Sea Salt** ☀
1 tsp. toasted **Sesame Seeds***

- In jar assemble dressing ingredients: oil, garlic, **Lemon Grass Vinegar** ☀, **Jerk Sauce** ☀, **Jerk Spice** ☀, and **Seasoned Sea Salt** ☀.
- About 20 minutes before serving toss broccoli with dressing** and chill.
- At serving time sprinkle with **Sesame Seeds**.

*To "toast" sesame seeds: in small pan, heat seeds over medium heat, stirring, until just lightly browned

** Do not marinate for more than 20 minutes — green colour will change

Herbal Biscuit Ring

1 tube refrigerator type Buttermilk
  biscuits*
1/3 c. melted unsalted butter
2 Tbs. **Presto Pesto** ☀**

* for larger amounts use 2 tubes
  of biscuits, double butter mix and
  adjust baking time.
Super Spice ☀**, Mixed Hearty
Herbs** ☀**, Mild Savory Herbs** ☀
and **Down Island Dill** ☀ make a
delicious variation

- Preheat oven to 450°.
- Melt butter in 9 inch round pan
  or baking dish.
- Mix **Presto Pesto** ☀ with butter.
- Separate biscuit sections (usu-
  ally 10 in tube).
- Dip each biscuit (both sides) into
  Presto Pesto ☀ mix.
- Arrange in circle in pan.
- Bake according to package
  directions (usually 450° for 10
  minutes) or until springy and
  golden brown.
- Cool slightly before inverting onto
  serving plate.

≈ These biscuits make tasty snack sandwiches. Split and fill with small
   slices of cold meat or with chicken, egg, tuna salad. Cut in half for
   hors d'oeuvres size.

Dessert Coffee Californian

for each serving:
2 tsp. **California Coffee Mix**
  (p. 24)
2/3 c. boiling water
whipped cream
grated **Spice Island Cocoa Ball** ☀

- Place mix in large coffee cup or mug.
- Add boiling water and stir until mix is dissolved.*
- Top with dollop of whipped cream.
- Top cream with grated **Spice Island Cocoa Ball** ☀.

*Add Rum or Coffee Liqueur if you wish a spirited dessert drink.

VIII

Celestial Snacks & Sumptuous Suppers

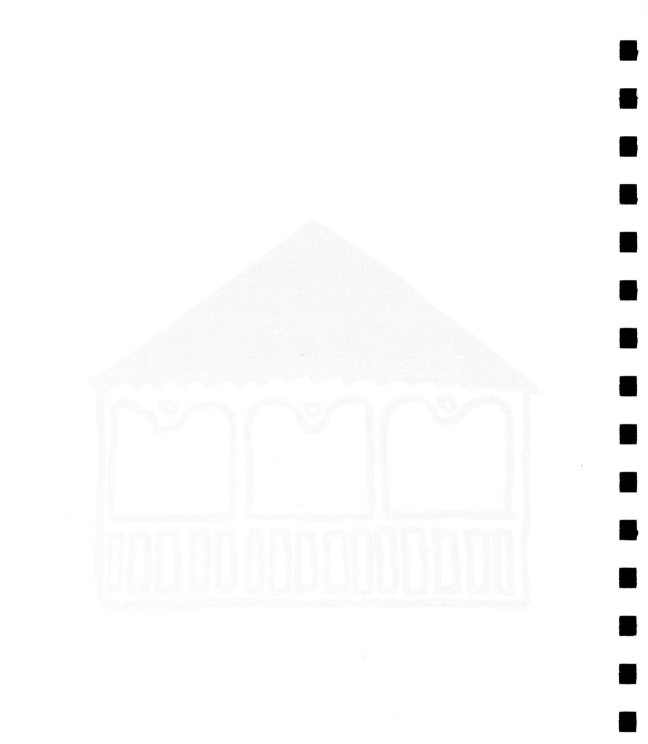

Dancing in the Moonlight

"Put on your high-heeled sneakers, we're steppin' out tonight." Dance to the beat of good old Rock 'n Roll, Bossanova and "Rhythm and Blues." Slow down the tempo for some romantic ballads and "Golden Oldies" … Swing with the Big Band Sound. The moon rises and lights the scene for an evening of dining, dancing and nostalgia.

Curried Carrot Soup

Teriyaki Steak Jamaican

Party Potatoes

Tomatoes Pyrenees

Southern Coffee

Serves 8

Curried Carrot Soup

4 Tbs. butter
1 medium yellow onion
1 tsp. minced garlic
2 tsp. **Caribbee Curry**
2 lbs. carrots, peeled and sliced
6 c. chicken bouillon
1 **Bouquet Garni**
1 c. milk
1/2 c. yogurt if serving cold
   or 1/2 c. cream if serving hot
Seasoned Sea Salt
Spiced Peppercorns, ground

- In large pot sauté onion and garlic until soft (but not brown).
- Add **Caribbee Curry** and cook 1 minute.
- Add carrots, bouillon and **Bouquet Garni**.
- Simmer for about 30 minutes until carrots are soft.
- Remove **Bouquet Garni** (squeezing out flavor).
- Purée in small batches, in food processor.
- Return to pot and add milk.
- To serve cold: blend in yogurt and chill until serving time.
- To serve hot: add cream and reheat.
- **Salt** and **pepper** to taste.
- Garnish each serving with chopped chives.

Teriyaki Steak Jamaican

5 – 6 lbs. top round steak cut 2
   inches thick

Marinade:
2 Tbs. **Sugar 'N' Spice** ☀
3 lg. cloves garlic minced
   (1-1/2 tsp.)
3 Tbs. sesame oil
1/2 c. **Ginger Garlic Vinegar** ☀
3 Tbs. **Jerk Sauce** ☀
1/4 tsp. **Ginger**

- Combine all marinade ingredients
in pan large enough to hold steak
(or steaks).
- Marinate, turning several times,
at room temperature for several
hours.
- Grill on rack, 5 – 6 inches from
flame. 10 – 12 min. a side for med-
rare (use meat thermometer).
- Remove from grill and let sit 10
minutes.
- Slice crosswise against grain
into thin slices.

Steak Spice Steak

This early **Sunny Caribbee** recipe from the "**Sunny Caribbee Dinner Party**"
folder is a delicious, distinctive menu option having less "heat" but more
"crunch".

5 – 6 lbs. sirloin or good quality
   top round steak cut 1-1/2 – 2 in.
   thick
water, **B-2** ☀ or soy sauce
Steak Spice ☀

- Moisten steak slightly with
water, **B-2** ☀ or soy sauce.
- Sprinkle both sides liberally with
Steak Spice ☀ pressing into
meat.
- Cook on outdoor grill. Following
directions for **Teriyaki Steak**
(above).

Party Potatoes

8 baking potatoes
lite oil
6 Tbs. butter
1 c. chopped onion
2 – 3 cloves garlic, minced
3/4 c. sour cream (lite)
1-1/2 tsp. **Seasoned Sea Salt**
   (or to taste)
1/2 tsp. **Herb Pepper**
1/2 tsp. **Mixed Hearty Herbs**
paprika

☾ Can be made ahead to here then refrigerate. Adjust reheating time.

- Preheat oven to 400°
- Wash potatoes well and pat dry.
- Rub skins with oil and prick in several places.
- Bake for approx. 1 hour.
- While potatoes are cooking, sauté onions and garlic in butter until tender (Do not brown!).
- When potatoes are done, slice piece off top length wise.
- Scoop out potato, leaving a potato skin shell.
- Mash the potato coarsely and mix with butter, onion, garlic, **Seasoned Sea Salt**, **Herb Pepper** and **Mixed Hearty Herbs**.
- Lightly restuff shells without packing too tightly and mounding top. Sprinkle with **Paprika**. ☾
- Place in baking pan and put in 375° oven.
- Bake until heated through (about 20 – 30 minutes).

Tomatoes Pyrenees

2 cloves minced garlic
2 Tbs. olive oil (lite)
2 Pts. cherry tomatoes
Presto Pesto ☀
Seasoned Sea Salt ☀
Herb Pepper ☀
1/4 c. chopped fresh parsley

- Sauté garlic lightly in oil. (Do not brown).
- Add tomatoes and cook only until skins start to burst (Don't overcook).
- Remove from heat and quickly sprinkle seasonings and fresh parsley over tomatoes.
- Gently toss to coat. ☾
- Serve immediately.

☾ Can do ahead: chill and serve, cold. If serving chilled, don't add parsley until serving time.

Southern Coffee

4 oz. bourbon
4 oz. cold strong coffee (**Tropical Blend** ☀ is good)
1 c. vanilla or coffee ice-cream
Nutmeg

- Blend all ingredients in blender (just until smooth don't overblend).
- Serve in demi-tasse cups.
- Sprinkle with freshly grated **Nutmeg**.

Make 2 batches to serve 8

Shooting Stars

Reach for the stars, make a wish and

never leave this magical place...

Boston Beach Chicken

Ratatouille de Midi - by Me

Ligurian Linguine

Garlic Croutons

Ginger-Ginger Speciale

Serves 6

Boston Beach Chicken

Boston Beach, on the northeast coast of Jamaica, is where "Jerking" originated and where it is still the best. The pungent aromas emanating from the tin roofed jerk-pit shanties, entice all to stop, explore and sample. Each "pit" proprietor claims to be the original, authentic and best and each one is probably right.

The craving for jerk has spread to every corner of Jamaica. Along the roads, and in the little villages, next to almost every "Red Stripe" sign, you'll find mobile steel drum "pits" and the entrepreneurs who have created Jamaica's first "fast food".

Indigenous pimento (allspice) is the prominent ingredient of this unique fare. The fragrant wood fuels the fire, and the berries are essential to the seasoning. My simple adaptation of "jerk chicken" has all the flavour and fire of the original...just turn on the grill and some Reggae and "every little ting gonna be alright."

6 whole chicken breasts split,
  skinned and boned
1/2 c. **Jerk Seasoning** ☀ (green)
1/4 c. cooking oil
Jerk Spice ☀

(In this menu cook ahead of time and refrigerate. Serve at room temperature.

- Mix **Jerk Seasoning** ☀ and oil in ziplock bag.
- Add chicken to bag. Squeeze out air and close.
- Marinate overnight in refrigerator, turning occasionally.
- Bring to room temperature before grilling.
- Shake off excess marinade and place on hot grill.
- Sprinkle with **Jerk Spice** ☀ if you want really torrid taste.
- Grill for 4-5 minutes a side uncovered. (
Serve hot or cold*

*Tangy Tropical Ting ☀, West Indian Green ☀ or Hot Pepper Jelly ☀ are complimentary condiments

Ratatouille de Midi – By Me

This is a real "no recipe" recipe because it depends what vegetables you have and how many you want to serve. I always make a lot because it is easy, it's good cold and makes a super filling for omelettes.* I don't first sauté veggies in oil the traditional way, which saves time, mess, calories and cholesterol. So here goes!

Vegetables:
  onions chopped in 1/2 inch pieces
  red and green peppers, 1 inch chop
  yellow summer squash, 1 inch chop
  zucchini, 1 inch chop
  tomatoes, coarsely chopped
  eggplant, 1/2 inch cubes
minced garlic to taste
1 or 2 **Bouquet Garni** ☀

Liquid:
  canned tomatoes with juice or V-8 or vegetable bouillon

Extra seasonings to taste:
  Seasoned Sea Salt ☀
  Herb Pepper ☀
  Mixed Hearty Herbs ☀

Parmesan cheese, grated

- Assemble vegetables, garlic, **Bouquet Garni** ☀ and liquid in large stock pot.
- Amount of liquid depends on amount and type of veggies. Start with about 2-1/2 inches in bottom of pot, add more if necessary.
- Bring all to boil, reduce heat, simmer covered, until veggies done but not mushy. Stir occasionally and check liquid.
- Adjust seasoning.
- Sprinkle servings with parmesan cheese.

Bonus: if you have a *lot* left over, and you've served it cold, and made omelettes; add more liquid, some pasta, adjust seasoning and sprinkle with cheese and/or **Croutons** (p. 155).

> **Benissimo ! . . . Instant Minestrone.**
>
> or . . .

Generously sprinkle with **Presto Pesto** ☀.

> **Voilà ! . . . Instant Soupe au Pistou.**

Ligurian Linguine

About 30 years ago, on my first trip to Italy, I discovered that there was more than just red sauce for "spaghetti" (the generic term for any "pasta" at that time). I had my first "green" sauce at a small, 3 table outdoor cafe in Portofino, an idyllic port on the Ligurian Coast. The aromas of basil, garlic, and cheeses wafting from the cavern within, seduced us all into our first "Pesto experience". Monuments, museums, cathedrals and gardens not withstanding, "Pesto" was and still is, one of my best memories of Italy

STEP I: Pronto Pesto Sauce

3 Tbs. extra virgin olive oil
3 Tbs. unsalted butter
1 – 2 cloves garlic minced and/or
   1 small shallot minced
1/4 c. **Presto Pesto** ☀
1/4 c. water
Seasoned Sea Salt ☀

STEP I I: Pasta Preparation

12 oz. pasta: linguine, angel hair, or
   vermicelli
Herbal Bread Crumbs*(p. 10) or
Garlic Croutons (next page)

Optional: additional chopped
   assorted fresh herbs: parsley,
   basil, dill, tarragon, chives for
   added colour and flavour

- In small sauce pan sauté garlic and/or shallot in oil and butter until soft, not brown.
- Add water and **Presto Pesto** ☀. Heat but do not boil and put aside.
- Add **Seasoned Sea Salt** ☀ to taste.

- Cook pasta "Al Dente," according to directions.
- Drain and place in warm serving bowl.
- Quickly toss with **Pesto Sauce**, coating evenly.
- Sprinkle with buttered **Herbal Bread Crumbs*** or **Garlic Croutons**.
- Add chopped fresh herbs for added colour and flavour.

Serves 6 as side dish**

* Sauté 1/4 c. **Herbal Bread Crumbs** (p. 13) in 1/2 Tbs. oil or butter over medium heat. Do not burn!

** For main dish, add small wedges of fresh tomatoes and/or crumbled cooked Italian Sausage.

Garlic Croutons

4 c. 1/2 in. cubes bread* (coarse
  homestyle, French or Italian
  bread is best)
2 cloves garlic, minced
4 Tbs. unsalted butter or Extra
  Virgin olive oil
Seasoned Sea Salt ☀

* vary size according to usage.

- Preheat oven to 350°.
- Put butter (or oil) and garlic in
  large bowl.
- Quickly toss bread crumbs in bowl
  to coat evenly.
- Place on baking sheet and bake
  for 15 minutes or until crisp and
  golden brown.
- Sprinkle lightly with **Seasoned
  Sea Salt** ☀.

Croutons add zest and interest to many dishes:

Soups: Garnish Gazpacho, Pea or Bean, Minestrone, Onion etc. with
  croutons;
Salads: an essential Caesar salad ingredient and an extra touch to other
  green, mixed or composed salads;
Casseroles and vegetables: sprinkle on top for extra flavour.

Ginger-Ginger Speciale

1 qt. vanilla ice cream or lemon
  sherbet
1/4 c. finely chopped Crystallized
  Ginger Gems ☀
Ginger Beer Syrup ☀

Optional: sliced pear, pineapple and
  peaches

- Place softened ice-cream in a
  bowl and swirl in **Ginger Gems** ☀.
- Mix well and return to freezer.
- Serve in glass goblets pouring
  small amount of ginger syrup over
  each and sprinkle with a few
  "Gems" or...
- Serve with sliced pears, pineapple, and peaches on dessert
  plate.

156

Super Summer Salad Supper

A hot and sultry night on the village green. After the band concert, a light and cool supper is the perfect ending to a harmonious evening with John Phillip Souza and some foot tapping, hand clapping "Dixieland."

"California Dreamin' " Curried Chicken Salad

Neptune Salad

Pesto Pasta Primavera Verde

Sicilian Salad

Pecan Butter Balls

Ginger Beer

"California Dreamin'" Curried Chicken Salad

Caribbee Curry Salad Dressing:*
  1/2 c. lite mayonnaise
  1-1/2 Tbs. **Caribbee Curry** ☀
  1 Tbs. **Chutney** ☀
  1/4 c. lite oil

4 c. cooked turkey or chicken
  breast cut into 1 inch cubes
1/2 c. celery cut large pieces
1/4 c. sliced scallions including
  green
1/2 c. blanched almonds or pecans
  coarsely chopped
1 c. large red or green seedless
  grapes halved
Additional fruit can be added:
  1 c. pineapple chunks, melon balls
  or mandarin or fresh orange
  pieces

- Combine all ingredients in blender or whisk briskly in bowl until creamy and well blended. Let mellow.
- Combine chicken, celery and scallions in large bowl.
- Add desired amount of **Curry Dressing*** to chicken mixture (enough to moisten well without being too "soupy").
- Chill until serving time (at least several hours to mellow flavours).
- Remove from fridge and add grapes, nuts and other fruits.
- Bring to cool room temperature before serving for best flavour.

*This is also a very appetizing dressing for egg salad.

≈ Left over dressing makes good fruit or veggie dip. Add a bit of low fat yogurt if too thick and some finely chopped nuts for fruit dip.

Perfectly Poached Chicken Breasts

Boned chicken breasts (at room
  temperature)
White wine or dry vermouth
Kuchela ☀**, or Jerk Seasoning** ☀
(green) or **Bouquet Garni** ☀

4 chicken breast halves yield
  approximately 4 c. cubes

- Place chicken breasts in pan and cover with water and several big splashes of wine.
- Add heaping Tbs. of **Kuchela** ☀, or **Jerk Seasoning** ☀ (green) or 1 **Bouquet Garni** ☀.
- Cover and bring to almost boiling.
- Simmer for 5 minutes then remove from heat.
- Let chicken sit in broth until cool (covered).
- Chicken will be very moist and not overcooked.

Neptune Salad

3 c. cooked fish (great way to use
   leftovers) salmon, sword fish,
   tuna, scallops or shrimp
1/4 c. capers
2 tsp. minced shallot
1/2 c. **Mild Savory Vinaigrette***
1/2 tsp. **Island Fish Spice** ☀
1 c. minced celery
mayonnaise
chopped chives and chopped
   parsley
Seasoned Sea Salt ☀ and **Herb
   Pepper** ☀

- Break fish into large chunk and
  place in bowl with capers and
  shallots.
- Add **Mild Savory Vinaigrette** and
  Island Fish Spice ☀ to bowl,
  tossing gently.
- Marinate all for 1/2 hour in
  refrigerator.
- Add celery and enough mayon-
  naise to moisten to your taste.
- Chives and parsley can be mixed
  in before serving.
- **Seasoned Sea Salt** ☀ and **Herb
  Pepper** ☀ to taste
- Serve in tomato cups, avocado
  halves or on lettuce.

***Mild Savory Vinaigrette:**
  3/4 c. oil
  1/4 c. **Lemon Grass Vinegar** ☀
  2 tsp. **Mild Savory Herbs** ☀
  1/2 tsp. **Seasoned Sea Salt** ☀
  1/2 tsp. **Herb Pepper** ☀

- Whisk all dressing ingredients
  briskly in a bowl or shake vigorously in glass jar. Let mellow
  before using.

〰 Two quick and easy ways to cook fish…and the leftovers are
   wonderful in **Neptune Salad:**

Blackened Fish à la Sunny Caribbee

1. Lightly coat fish (steaks or fillets) with mayonnaise. Liberally sprinkle
Island Fish Spice ☀ over both sides. Broil at highest heat quickly until
just done.*
2. Fish may also be dipped in butter, sprinkled with **Island Fish Spice** ☀
and quickly cooked in very hot cast iron pan.

* Do not overcook — fish is done as soon as transparency in center
   disappears.

Pesto Pasta Primavera Verde

Presto Pesto Dressing:
  3/4 c. extra virgin olive oil
  1/4 c. **Lemon Grass Vinegar** ☀
  1/2 tsp. **Seasoned Sea Salt** ☀
  2 Tbs. **Presto Pesto** ☀
  2 lg. cloves garlic minced
  1/4 c. mayonnaise

1 lb. Fusilli (shells, tortellini or
  Penne also good choices)
Vegetables:
  broccoli flowerettes
  beans
  asparagus
  green peas or sugar snaps
  celery
  zucchini
  green onions-scallions
  cucumbers (seeded)
  chopped fresh herbs parsley,
    chives, basil

- Whisk all ingredients in a bowl or shake vigorously in covered jar.
- Let mellow before using.

- Prepare pasta of your choice according to instructions.
- Drain and set aside.
- Cut vegetables in large bite size pieces: broccoli, beans, asparagus, peas should be blanched for a few minutes.
- Combine prepared vegetables with pasta in a large bowl.
- Add sufficient **Presto Pesto Dressing** to moisten well.
- Chill.
- Add 1/4 c. mayonnaise and more dressing if necessary, before serving.
- Adjust seasoning with dash of **Presto Pesto** ☀ if needed and fresh herbs.

Sicilian Salad

Two 20 oz. cans garbanzos
   (chickpeas)
1/2 lb. salami julienned
1/2 red onion cut in medium dice
1/4 c. sliced scallion whites
   (reserve greens)
1 clove garlic minced
1 c. chopped red and/or green
   pepper
1/2 c. small green or black brine
   cured olives, pitted
1/2 c. chopped fresh fennel
1/4 c. olive oil
1 Tbs. **Lemon Grass Vinegar** ☀
2 tsp. **Mixed Hearty Herbs** ☀
1 tsp. **Oregano**
sliced scallion greens
1 c. 1/4 inch provolone cubes
Seasoned Sea Salt ☀ (to taste)
ground **Spiced Peppercorns** ☀
   (to taste)

☾ Can be made day before.

- Drain beans and put in large bowl
  with salami, onion, scallion, garlic
  pepper, olives, and fennel.
- Combine oil, **Lemon Grass
  Vinegar** ☀ and **seasonings** and
  pour over all.
- Marinate, in refrigerator for
  several hours, gently tossing
  occasionally. ☾
- Just before serving mix in cheese
  cubes and scallion greens.
- Adjust **seasoning**.

Salad Savoir Faire

You can make exciting international salads with a few basic ingredients in your fridge, pantry and freezer. Be prepared:

Basics: tomatoes, onions, peppers, greens, plus zucchini and cucumbers and **Sunny Caribbee Salad Dressings.**

Mexican: Add chicken or beef strips, shell beans, avocado, hot peppers, shredded cheddar, top with sour cream and prepared **Salsa** p. 76 (or **Simple Super Spice Dressing** p. 52).

Nicoise: Add shrimp or tuna, capers, hard boiled egg, boiled small potatoes, green beans, brine cured black olives (**Sauce Verte** p. 65).

Greek: Add feta cheese, black olives (preferably calamata), cucumber, more **Oregano** (**Mixed Hearty Vinaigrette** p. 167).

French: Add chicken, artichoke hearts, baby zucchini, crumbled chèvre cheese, mushrooms (**Mild Savory Vinaigrette** p. 159).

Italian: add provolone, mozzarella, or parmesan cheese, prosciutto, salami, or sausage pieces, green olives, pimiento, fennel (**Presto Pesto Dressing** p. 160).

West Indian: Add pineapple, mango, papaya or banana, chicken or pork pieces, coconut, almonds or cashews (**Fog City Salad Dressing** p. 59, or **Curry Dressing** p. 158).

Asian: Add chicken, beef, pork, or shrimp, snow peas, water chestnut, sprouts, almonds, bamboo shoot, **Sesame Seeds** (**Sesame Dressing** p. 139, or **Curry Dressing** p.158) .

≈ These salads are best composed on individual plates but they can also be nicely arranged in a bowl "Tossed salad", "Cobb salad" or "Chef salad " style.

Ginger Beer

a very cooling and refreshing hot night drink

for each glass:
2-3 Tbs. **Ginger Beer Syrup** ☀
8 oz. club soda
lemon slice
mint sprigs

- Put syrup in glass and mix well with soda. (amount varies according to your taste).
- Add ice cubes, a lemon slice and garnish with mint.

Pecan Butter Balls

1/2 c. butter
2 tsp. **West Indian Honey** ☀
1 c. flour
1/4 tsp. salt
1 tsp. **Vanilla-Vanilla** ☀
3/4 c. chopped pecans

- Preheat oven to 300°.
- Cream butter and **W.I. Honey** ☀.
- Add remaining ingredients and mix thoroughly. Chill.
- Form into small balls. Place on cookie sheet.
- Bake 30 – 35 min. Cool.
- Roll in powdered sugar.

164

Grand Finale Fondue

This is it! The *grand finale* menu of "Sunshine Style." It could also be the grand finale supper for the last day of summer, the sailing trip or skiing...for the final game or show of the season... graduation...or a great day anywhere.

Beef Fondue

Fondue Sauces

Insalata Mista

Crusty Bread

Celebration Ice Cream Pie
with Spice Island Chocolate Sauce

Serves 8

Beef Fondue

Having skied for years on the cold and icy slopes of New England, we ventured forth one year to St. Anton, Austria to enjoy the Tyrolean sunshine. There, we first experienced classic "**Fondue Bourguignonne**". We were so taken with this "event" that we purchased all the essential paraphernalia, enabling us to repeat the performance at home. For ever after, **Fondue** has been our traditional "rite of passage" for birthday celebrants. It is a casual, congenial and festive happening which allows everyone to do their own thing.

3 lbs. beef tenderloin

Fondue Sauces

peanut oil

fondue forks or wooden handled
  skewers

various sauces and
  accompaniments

- Cut beef into bite size chunks (about 1 inch) and place on a platter.
- Put sauces in serving bowls.
- Fill fondue pot about 3/4 full with peanut oil.
- Heat oil on stove and then place over fondue burner (or follow manufacturer's instructions).
- Each person spears their fork with beef (not more than 2 cubes) and cooks in oil until desired doneness (be sure to keep oil hot).
- Dip into your choice of sauces.

No Cook-No Work Fondue Sauces:

Tangy Tropical Ting ☀
West Indian Green ☀
Caribbee Hot Sauce ☀
Chutney ☀
Island Nutmeg Mustard ☀
Spicee Catsup ☀
Chopped onion
Chopped peanuts

Variations with a little work:
Tzatziki (p. 124)
Pesto Power Dip (p. 33)
Spicee Catsup mixed with chopped
  onion
Caribbee Curry ☀, or **Down Island
Dill** ☀ and sour cream (1-1/2 Tbs.
  seasoning to 1 c. sour cream)
Savoury Hollandaise (p. 13)

Insalata Mista

a simple, uncomplicated green salad with a simple dressing, that lets the varied and true flavours of mixed greens predominate, especially good with rich dishes that have complex flavours.

Mixed greens or mesclun
  (see p. 65)
Mixed Hearty Vinaigrette*:
  3/4 c. oil
  1/4 c. **Lemon Grass Vinegar** ☀
  1-1/2 tsp. **Mixed Hearty Herbs** ☀
  2 cloves garlic, minced
  1 tsp. Dijon mustard
  1/2 tsp. sugar
  1/2 tsp. **Herb Pepper** ☀
  1/2 tsp. **Seasoned Sea Salt** ☀

- Assemble in salad bowl a variety of greens with different colours, textures and flavours.
- Toss lightly before serving with just enough dressing to lightly coat greens.
- Add additional **Seasoned Sea Salt** ☀ and **Herb Pepper** ☀ to taste.

*or **Presto Pesto Dressing** (p. 160)

Cheese and/or **Garlic Croutons** (see p. 155) can be sprinkle on individual servings if you need an added touch.

Various Vinaigrette Ventures

When you have the Vinaigrette and not much time:

1. Toss vinaigrette with leftover pasta, potaotes, rice or whatever left-over vegetables, meat or fish that you have to make simple, inventive salads.
2. Brush on baguette slices to make **Crostini** or toss with bread cubes to make **Croutons**.
3. Create a quick marinade for meat poultry or fish.
4. Toss with raw chopped vegetables.
5. Marinate slices of fresh Mozzarella or Chèvre cheese for appetizer salads or cocktail hors d'oeuvres.

Celebration Ice Cream Pie

Step I:
1 baked 9 in. pastry shell
1 qt. ice cream softened*

Step II: Meringue:
4 egg whites
1/2 tsp. **Vanilla-Vanilla** ☀
1/4 tsp. cream of tartar
1/2 c. sugar

* Combinations are good here:
Layer chocolate, vanilla, strawberry or coffee, vanilla and
orange sherbet or raspberry
sherbet and butter pecan. Use
your favourites!

❨ Can be made ahead to here,
returned to freezer and browned
before serving.

Step I:
• Spread softened ice-cream in pie
shell.
• Put in freezer until meringue is
ready.

Step II:
• Beat egg white with **Vanilla-
Vanilla** ☀ and cream of tartar
until soft peak stage.
• Gradually add sugar continuing
to beat until whites very stiff.

Step III:
• Spread **Meringue** over ice cream
(from edge to center), complete
covering and sealing edge of
pastry. ❨
• Bake at 475° for 2 – 3 minutes
or until **Meringue** is browned.
• Serve with **Spice Island Chocolate Sauce** (see next page)

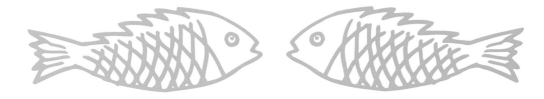

Spice Island Chocolate Sauce

4 oz. grated **Spice Island Cocoa Balls** ☀ (approx. 4)
3/4 c. water
1 c. sugar
dash salt
6 tbs. margarine or butter
1 tsp. **Vanilla-Vanilla** ☀
(1 Tbs. dark rum can be added)

- In pan heat grated **Spice Island Cocoa Balls** ☀ and water over low heat. Stirring constantly until chocolate is smooth.
- Stir in sugar and dash of salt.
- Simmer until slightly thick (about 5 minutes).
- Remove from heat and blend in 6 Tbs. margarine or butter and 1 tsp. **Vanilla-Vanilla** ☀.

Guest Quarters

Since the beginning, countless **Sunny Caribbee** customers, friends and fans have contributed an abundance of ideas, recipes and moral support to our pursuit of the "Paradise Plan". This section is dedicated to all these people who continuously keep us motivated and challenged.

Selecting the guest recipes was no easy task! From the extensive accumulated collection, I had to determine which recipes were the most original, distinctive, and creative while exemplifying the simplicity and taste of **Sunshine Style**.

Interestingly, the majority of contributions seemed to anticipate the theme of the "yet to come" book and the healthy way people like to eat today – chicken, fish, rice and beans, vegetables and fruits being the preferred foods. Unfortunately, the sameness of concepts presented numerous duplications and/or similarities. We received several "Curry in a Hurry" and "Presto Pesto Pasta" recipes that were already in our shop "Handout" collection as well as other nearly identical contributions. Therefore, your recipe may not have been included.

The Guest Quarters Recipes are original, as written by contributors and are not edited or any way changed by me, unless specifically noted.

It's fun to hear from you so keep those letters and calls coming!

Appetizers

Soups

Breads

Meat & Poultry

Fish

Potatoes, Pasta, Rice, Vegetables

Salads/Dressings

Sauces

Jerk Dip or Sauce

1 T. **Jerk Seasoning** ☀, 1 t. **Herb Pepper** ☀, 1/2 t. **Seasoned Sea Salt** ☀

1/2 c. sour cream (If thicker dip is desired: 1/3 c. sour cream and 1/4 c. cottage cheese.)

Mix all ingredients together and serve with slices of carrot, celery, bell pepper, zucchini, cucumber and flowerets of cauliflower and broccoli, etc. This also works well with Water Crackers or a similar type of cracker.

If this dip is thinned with one or two teaspoons of milk, it may be used as a salad dressing.   *Jeanne Bach-Clark, Tortola, BVI*

Bara

This Indian recipe traveled from Trinidad with Chan, one of our staff, who cooks many other exotic treats for us including Rotis and **Mango Chutney** ☀.

Mango Chutney ☀
1/2 lb. yellow split peas
1/2 lb. spinach
1/2 lb. flour
1 Tbs. **Herb Pepper** ☀
1 Tsp. **Turmeric**
Seasoned Sea Salt ☀ to taste
1 lg. onion
4 cloves garlic
1 small hot pepper
1 package dry yeast

Soak split peas overnight. Puree in food processor to make a paste. Coarsely chop spinach in food processor. Blend all ingredients to make a batter. Add yeast and make into balls or small flat patties and deep fry until batter cooked and light brown. These go well with traditional dip of green mango minced finely with garlic and onion. Salt and pepper to taste.

Chanardaye Davis, Tortola, BVI

Dodie's Borscht

2 cans "Harvard" beets*
2 TBS butter
1/2 c chopped celery
1/2 c chopped onion
2 cans consommé**
2 cans water
1 Tbs **Down Island Dill** ☀
1 c sour cream
1 Tbs lemon juice
Seasoned Sea Salt ☀ to taste

*can substitute pickled beets

Sauté celery and onions in butter until soft. Add beets and consommé and water to pan and simmer uncovered for 30 min. Add **Down Island Dill** ☀ and sour cream. Blend, in batches. Add lemon juice. Chill. Serve in glass bowls and garnish with sour cream and sprigs of dill.

Dodie Phillips, Kennebunk Beach, ME

can substitute beef bouillon and simmer with **Bouquet Garni ☀ —ed.

Creole Peanut Soup

Roz's restaurant "Carib Casseroles" was one of my Tortola favourites. It has been closed for several years, but I am fortunate to have this renowned recipe. – ed.

In a large saucepan, sauté 2 medium onions (minced) in 2 Tbs. oil, until soft. Add 2 Tbs. flour and cook over low heat for 2 minutes. Remove from heat. In a bowl, combine 3 c. milk with 3/4 c. peanut butter, and 1 tsp. **BBQ Seasoning** ☀. Combine with onions and cook until smooth. Do not boil. Add 3 c. tomato juice and 1 Tbs. **Spicee Catsup** ☀ and mix well. Serve slightly chilled.

Roz Griffiths, Roadtown, Tortola, BVI

** Adjust seasonings with **Seasoned Sea Salt** ☀ and a few grinds of **Spiced Peppercorns** ☀ and perhaps a dash of **West Indian Rum Peppers** ☀. – ed.*

Cold Curried Pea Soup

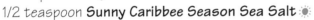

1 can strong chicken broth

1 package frozen peas

1 tablespoon chopped chives or scallion stalks

1 teaspoon lemon juice

1 teaspoon **Curry Powder***

1/2 teaspoon **Sunny Caribbee Season Sea Salt** ☀

1/4 teaspoon **Spiced Peppercorns** ☀

1/2 cup yogurt

Garnish: chopped chives

In a small saucepan, bring broth to a boil. Add peas, bring to a boil again; cover and simmer for 10 minutes.

Add the chives, lemon juice, **Curry, Salt,** and **Pepper**, and pureé in food processor.

Chill for 4 to 6 hours or overnight.

Add yogurt and serve garnished with chives. Serves 4.

Joan F. Quillen, Palm Beach and Tortola, BVI

** I suggest 1 Tbs. **Caribbee Curry** ☀. Thin with milk if too thick and adjust seasonings. – ed.*

Lorna's Classy Tomato Soup

1 can cream of tomato soup
1 soup can of orange juice
1 soup can of cream*
1-1/2 oz. (3 Tbs.) Cointreau
1 Tbs. **Ginger Beer Syrup**

   Whisk all the ingredients until well blended. Chill. Garnish each serving with chopped chives. Makes 4 large or 6 small servings.

Judith Sura, Beaconsfield, P.Q. Canada

*Use lite milk to reduce fat and calories. Soup will be thinner, however. – ed

Sunny Caribbee Turkey Meat Balls

With the new consciousness about cholesterol, turkey has become a hot commodity in the north. One of my favorite recipes is for **Sunny Caribbee Turkey Meat Balls:**

1.5 pounds of ground turkey
1 medium onion
Bread crumbs
2 very liberal shakes of **West Indian Green**
1 TSP **Herb Pepper**

Finely chop medium onion. Combine in large mixing bowl the onion, the 1.5 pounds of ground turkey, 1 TSP **Herb Pepper** and 2 very liberal shakes of **West Indian Green**. Mix with your hands and add bread crumbs until consistency is good for forming meat balls. Form meat balls and fry in pan lightly covered with olive oil. When meat balls are golden brown on all sides remove and drain off excess oil on plate covered with paper towels. When meat balls have drained add to the cooked sauce. Raise heat and cook uncovered for about another 30 minutes, checking for sauce consistency. After finished, let stand for about 10 minutes and then cook up your favorite pasta and have a feast.

Gail McCloskey Middleton, Staten Island, NY

Pasta Red Sauce

Two 16 oz cans of Italian plum tomatoes

1 small can tomato paste

2 large white onions

3 cloves of garlic

1 TBS. S.C. **Herb Pepper**

1 TBS **Oregano**

1/2 TBS **Thyme**

2 liberal shakes of **Caribbee Hot Sauce** ☀

Red Wine to taste

Olive Oil to cover bottom of cooking pot

Finely chop onions and garlic. Cover interior bottom of cooking pot with olive oil and place on low flame. Add chopped onions and garlic. Cook covered on low heat stirring occasionally. When mixture is translucent add juice from the canned plum tomatoes. Before you add plum tomatoes coarsely chop them. Add plum tomatoes to cooking mixture. Add tomato paste stir. Cover and let cook for about 15 minutes (stirring whenever). Then add **Herb Pepper** ☀, **Oregano, Thyme, Caribbee Hot Sauce** ☀ and Red Wine. Stir until all seasons are blended and then cook for about 1 hour in partially covered pot. Constantly stir and check so sauce doesn't burn. If sauce reduces too much add more red wine.

This is my basic red sauce recipe. Into the sauce you can add the following (when sauce is done): Sunny Caribbee Turkey Meat Balls (p. 175).

Gail McCloskey Middleton, Staten Island, NY

Lisa's Curry in a Hurry

1/4 c. butter

1 large onion sliced

1/2 c. chopped celery

3 c. cubed , cooked chicken breast

1 can cream of chicken soup

1 c. yoghurt

1/2 tsp. **Coriander**, 1 Tbs. **Curry Powder**, 2 Tbs. **Caribbee Curry**

In large skillet, sauté onion and celery until translucent (about 5 min). Stir in 1 Tbs. **Curry Powder** and **Coriander**. Cover and cook 5 min. (medium heat) add chicken and 1 Tbs. **Caribbee Curry**. Stir, cover, simmer 5 min. Add soup, yoghurt and last 1 Tbs. **Caribbee Curry**. Cook until just bubbling. Serve over rice. (Brown rice especially good!)

Mango Chutney is a traditional Accompaniment.

Lisa Gunter Fresne, Millerton, NY

Roast Pork Tenderloin

A mother and daughter recipe

1 c. chicken stock

1/4 c. **Tangy Tropical Ting**

1 tsp. **B-2 Sauce**

1/4 c. **West Indian Honey**

1 Tbs. lemon juice

1 – 2 cloves crushed garlic

2 tsp. **Chinese Five Spice**

3 pork tenderloins

2 Tbs. corn starch

Combine marinade ingredients. Marinate pork tenderloins for 2 hours, turning occasionally*. Coat meat with corn starch, after removing from marinade. Place in shallow roasting pan: bake at 325° for 45 minutes**, basting frequently.

Louise MacAuliffe, Vero Beach, FL
Mona Brewer, New Smyrna Beach, FL

*marinate in ziplock bags

**check doneness with meat thermometer – ed.

Bar-B-Que Chicken Caribbee

serves 4

4 chicken breast halves, skin removed

2 – 12 oz. beers

4 TBS. **Caribbee Jerk Seasoning** ☀

1 orange, juice only

4 TBS. Teriyaki Sauce*

Combine all ingredients in large bowl. Add chicken. Chill for 2 to 4 hours. Prepare Bar-B-Que. On grill cook 4-5 minutes, meat side down. Turn and cook 10 more minutes. Turn again and cook meat side 3-5 minutes at an angle to the first grill marks to get a criss-cross effect. Serve with your favorite side dishes.

Mark Deutman, Encinitou, CA

P.S. The same can be done with fish. Alter cooking time to 4-5 minutes per side total.

I suggest **Jerk Sauce ☀ – ed.*

Shrimp Curry Spudzle

1 lb. shrimp-raw-shelled

1 cup celery sliced

1 cup onions diced

1 cup sour cream

Caribbee Curry ☀ to taste - 1 Tbsp or more

Heat fry pan & add two or three Tbsp of olive oil. Sauté celery & onions, stirring till half done. Add shrimp, keep stirring. Add **Caribbee Curry** ☀. When shrimp are mostly pink, add sour cream. A small amount of chicken broth may be added to thin the sauce. Taste and add more **Curry** to your liking. A little fresh grated ginger may be added also. Do not over cook the shrimp. It will get tough & dry. Serve with **Caribbean Curried Rice**.

Noonie Crabtree, Itasca, IL

Caribbee Fish Brochettes

1-1/2 LB white fish
1/2-1 yellow onion (mild)
1-2 TBLS **Island Fish Spice** ☀
4 TBLS olive oil
2 TBLS lemon juice

Cut fish into 1 inch squares or cubes. Combine remaining ingredients and pour over fish cubes and marinate at least 2 hours (or overnight). Grill fish on skewers until opaque or lightly browned on all sides.

Megan Delaney, Costa Mesa CA

Tortola Tunafish Sandwiches

(serving: 4 sandwiches)
1 – 4 oz. can fancy albacore
1 heaping tbl mayonnaise (or enough to moisten)
1 tsp-1 Tbs. **Caribbee Hot Sauce** ☀ (what you can handle)*
*Mix well together the above ingred. in a bowl.
Add:
 1/4 c. thinly sliced celery
1 tbl sweet relish
1 tbl sunflower seeds (buy already shelled)
1-2 tbl chopped **Cilantro**
thinly sliced green onion (white part only)

*Mix well. Spread on toasted wheat bread top with lettuce leaf (optional avocado slices x 2) and add remaining 2nd half of toast wheat bread to make a sandwich.

Denney Verhaege, San Diego, CA

Jeanne Bach-Clark uses **Bloody Mary Magic** ☀ *(1 TBS-for 6-1/2 oz can tuna) In tuna salad. She also suggests serving Tuna Salad in avocado or tomato halves – ed.*

Island Fish Spice Fry

2t. **Island Fish Spice** ☀
2t. **Herb Pepper** ☀
2t. **Mild Savory Herbs** ☀
1/4 c. flour
1/4c. bread crumbs
4 med. fish filets or steaks
1 egg
2T. water
peanut or olive oil for frying

Combine first five ingredients and blend. Rinse, trim fish as needed. Whip together egg and water, and dip fish into it coating both sides. Then coat each piece with the spiced mixture. Fry in med.-hot oil just until cooked. Do NOT overcook. Serves 4. (Extra spice mixture may be refrigerated or frozen and saved for next fish fry meal.) Fish may also be baked in lightly greased baking pan 350deg. for 10-20 min. depending upon thickness.

Jeanne Bach-Clark, Tortola BVI

Jeanne's Caribbee Banana French Toast

Serves 6, using 1 egg per person
6 eggs
1 Tbs. S.C. **Sugar n' Spice** ☀
1 tsp. S.C. Pure **Vanilla-Vanilla** ☀
3 Tbs. milk
2 ripe bananas
1 tsp. "plus" corn oil
12 standard size slices whole wheat bread or favorite bread

Whip eggs with fork or whisk in straight-sided bowl; add next three ingredients and mix. Add banana by 1-inch chunks & mash against side of bowl with fork. Stir. Dip bread slices one at a time into mix; turn to coat both sides. Do not soak.

Sauté in 8-10-inch teflon type fry pan in 1 tsp. oil. After each batch in pan (every set of 3 or 4 slices browned on each side), add additional 1 tsp. oil to fry next batch.

Serve with maple syrup &/or powdered sugar. Sprinkle with **Sunny Caribbee Fresh Ground Nutmeg.**

Jeanne Bach-Clark, Tortola BVI

Caribbee Pineapple Bread

1 c. crushed, undrained pineapple
    (8-1/2 oz. can)
1/2 c. raisins
1/4 c. **Sugar Crystals***
2 c. self rising flour
1 c. chopped walnuts
1 c. **Sugar N Spice** ☀
1/4 c. butter or margarine,
    softened
2 eggs
*Plantation Sugar ☀

Combine and stir first three ingredients together. Set aside in a small bowl. Combine next two ingredients and set aside. Now put last three ingredients into mixing bow and blend well. add flour mixture alternately with pineapple mixture. When completely blended, put into greased loaf pan. Bake 350 degrees for 30-45 min.

Jeanne Bach-Clark, Tortola BVI

Sunny Seas-R's Salad

1 Med. head Romaine lettuce
1/3 c. olive oil
1/4 c. S.C. **Lime Vinegar** ☀
1 egg
2 tsp. **Sunny Caribbee Herb Pepper** ☀
1/2 tsp. **Sunny Caribbee Seasoned Sea Salt** ☀
Squeeze of 4-in to 6 inches of anchovy paste
    (varies according to taste)
1/3 c. to 1/2 c. ground parmesan
3/4 c. croutons

Cut core from Romaine lettuce. Wash each lettuce leaf and shake excess water off.* Combine next six ingredients in a covered jar. Shake vigorously and set aside.

In 2-qt. bowl, tear each romaine leaf into pieces; this will nearly fill the bowl. Then pour oil mixture in a circle over the lettuce and with tongs. Gently toss to coat leaves. Finally, add croutons and sprinkle parmesan cheese over salad and toss lightly to evenly distribute all ingredients. Serves 6 for dinner or 4 for luncheon salads. Serve with hot **S.C. Herbal Pita Toasts** (p. 46).

Jeanne Bach-Clark, Tortola BVI

Use salad spinner dryer – ed.
Classic Caesar dressing includes garlic as an ingredient – ed.

Jeanne's Marmalade Dressing

1/2 c. **Sunny Caribbee Marmalade** ☀

2 Tbs. **S.C. Spicee Catsup** ☀

2 Tbs. **S.C. Ginger Garlic Vinegar** ☀

2 Tbs. water

1 tsp. **S.C. Sugar 'n' Spice** ☀

Combine all above ingredients and stir with a fork until well blended. Serve over torn romaine lettuce topped with cubed or sliced avocado, diagonal cuts of celery, and sprinkling of sliced green onion. (Note: rind may need to be strained from dressing if rind is not soft.) Serves 4-6 salads.

Jeanne Bach-Clark, Tortola, BVI

Caribbean Coleslaw

1 head shredded cabbage

1 Bermuda onion-thinly sliced

1 teaspoon minced garlic

1 tablespoon **Sunny Caribbee Sugar 'n' Spice** ☀

1/4 teaspoon yellow **Caribbee Hot Sauce** ☀

juice of 1 lemon

1 red bell pepper-diced

1 Cup mayonnaise

1 tablespoon olive oil

1 tablespoon cane vinegar (wine vinegar may be used)*

Combine in large bow and let stand in refrigerator for a few hours.

Chris Pranis, Moriches, NY

* I suggest **Lemon Grass Vinegar** ☀ – ed.

Road Town Ranch Dressing

1 Tbsp. **Herb-Pepper Blend** ☀

1 Cup Light Mayonnaise (Hellman's)

2 Tbsp. Vinegar*

Blend ingredients until smooth & creamy. Refrigerate. Great as a salad dressing or as a marinade to brush on for grilled poultry or fish.

A contribution for the Sunny Carribee Cookbook, from:

Ginger Barnett, Humboldt, KS

Try a **Sunny Caribbee Vinegar** ☀ – maybe **Lime** – ed.

Nutmeg Mustard Vinaigrette

3/4 Tablespoon **Nutmeg Mustard** ☀   **Seasoned Sea Salt** ☀

1 teaspoon plain mustard   **Herb Pepper** ☀

1/4 cup white wine vinegar*   1 cup olive oil

Whisk both mustards and the white wine vinegar together. Add Seasoned Sea Salt and Herb Pepper to taste (usually close to a teaspoon of each). Drizzle the olive oil in a steady stream, whisking vigorously.

Conni Gallo, Lakewood, CO

*I suggest **Lemon Grass** ☀ or **Ginger Garlic** ☀ – ed.

Gena's Chicken Marinade

4 chicken breasts, boned & skinned
1/2 cup Italian dressing
2-3 cloves chopped garlic
1/4 cup Sunny Caribbee Yellow **Hot Sauce** ☀

Let marinade over night. Throw on the barbecue grill. Absolutely delicious & easy!!

Gina Henderson, Seattle, WA

P.S. For your upcoming cookbook!

Papaya Sauce for Ham

Mix:
1/2 jar of **Sunny Caribbee Papaya Jam** ☀*
1 cup brown sugar**
1/4 cup pineapple juice
4 slices pineapple

Score a 5 lb. ham. Cover with mixture of jam, sugar and juice. Cook 2 hours in a 350° over. The last half hour of cooking top ham with pineapple slices

*Tamarind ☀ or **Passionfruit Jam** ☀ can be used in place of **Papaya** ☀.

Mr. & Mrs. D. Daniel, Colorado Springs, CO

I suggest using 1/4 c. **Sugar 'N' Spice ☀ and 3/4 c. brown sugar — ed.

Nutmeg Mustard-Caper Sauce

Serve over grilled meat, chicken...even mild fish!

1 Tablespoon butter or margarine

4 teaspoons steak sauce

2 Tablespoons sherry

1-1/4 teaspoons **Nutmeg Mustard** ☀

3/4 teaspoon plain mustard

1/4 teaspoon Worcestershire

1 Tablespoon capers

Dash **Herb Pepper** ☀

Heat butter or margarine. Stir in remaining ingredients and heat covered till sauce simmers. Pour over steak, chicken or fish.

Conni Gallo, Lakewood, CO

Nelda's Caribbee Rum Sauce

1/2 c. **Sunny Caribbee Sugar 'n' Spice** ☀

1/2 c. butter

1/4 c. dark rum

1 egg

In 1-qt. saucepan melt butter and blend in Sugar 'n' Spice over medium heat. Add rum and remove from heat. Whip egg in cup and slowly pour into butter mix, stirring constantly as egg is poured into hot mix.

Serve over a variety of cakes: pound, banana, spice, angelfood; or may be served over chilled sliced fruit, ice cream, or vanilla pudding. Top with flower-squirt of whipped cream.

Nelda Kilbride, North Sound, Virgin Gorda

Caribbee Barbecue Sauce

Carefree and Quick, Hot and Spicy for: Hamburg, Steak, Chops, Ribs, Chicken

Mix 1/3 c **Spicee Catsup** ☀ with 1-1/2 tsp. **Caribbee Hot Sauce** ☀. Add 1 tbs. salad oil. Thin to desired consistency with water, wine or vinegar. (**Ginger-Garlic Vinegar** ☀ especially good.) An added touch: Dash of **Seasoned Sea Salt** ☀, **Steak Spice** ☀, or **Jerk Spice** ☀.

Greg Gunter, Tortola, BVI

Honey-Ginger Dipping Sauce

(for chicken or pork)

1 TBS. **West Indian Honey** ☀

1 TBS **B-2 Sauce** ☀

1 TBS **Jerk Spice** ☀

1/4 c. **Ginger Beer Syrup** ☀

1/4 c. **Tamarind Jam** ☀

1/2 c. water

1 tsp corn starch

Combine: **Honey** ☀, **B-2** ☀, **Jerk** ☀, **Ginger Beer Syrup** ☀, **Jam** ☀, and water. Bring to boil. Simmer for a few minutes. Dissolve corn starch in water and gradually add to sauce, cooking and stirring constantly until thick.   *Anonymous*

Boursin Gratin

3 # small red potatoes, unpeeled

2 c. heavy cream

1/3 c **S.C. Boursin** (p. 96)

serves 8

* I suggest boiling potatoes for a minute before layering to assure evenly cooked potatoes – ed.

- Butter 9x13 baking dish
- Scrub and thinly slice potatoes*
- Mix cream and **Boursin** in large pan over medium heat 'til smooth
- Butter baking dish
- Place half of potatoes in dish in rows slightly overlapping
- Sprinkle lightly with salt
- Pour half of **Boursin** mix over potatoes
- Arrange remaining potatoes in same manner
- Sprinkle with salt and pour remaining **Boursin** mix overall
- Bake at 400° for about 1 hr. until top golden brown & potatoes tender
- Garnish with chopped parsley and/or other herbs

Lisa Gunter Fresne, Millerton, NY

Jerk Rice

2c. water

2t. **Jerk Seasoning** , Dry

1/2t. **Seasoned Sea Salt**

1/2 T. **Herb Pepper**

1-2 T. olive oil

1 c. long grain 20-min. rice

1/2 med. onion, diced

1/2 med. green or red pepper, diced

Add first four ingredients together in 2-qt. sauce pan and bring to boil. Meanwhile, sauté onion and pepper in oil. Add to seasoned water with rice when water boils Cook over low heat until water is absorbed, about 15-20 min. Serves 4. May add more zip, with a dash or two of **Tangy Tropical Ting**.

Optional addition:
1/2 can (16-oz.) favorite beans with another teaspoon of **Jerk Seasoning**, Dry*

Jeanne Bach-Clark, Tortola, BVI

*With the addition of meat (beef, sausage, pork or chicken), this becomes a Jamaican main dish called "Dirty Rice" — ed.

Greg's Curried Onions*

Quarter 1 medium onion per person. Wrap each onion in foil. Before closing foil, add to each pack:

1 tsp. butter

1 heaping tsp. **Caribbee Curry**

Close foil securely. Cook on grill or in hot oven for 20-30 minutes. Serve in foil.

Greg Gunter, Tortola, BVI

*See p. 126 for alternative **Presto Pesto** or **Steak Spice Onions** — ed.

Dear Sir:

I have this really great recipe for unusual mashed potatoes. It's very Islandy, and it is Very, Very Sunny Caribbee. I wish to submit it for consideration in your coming soon cookbook.

Sunny Caribbee Spice Island Mashed

It goes like this;

6-medium Idaho potatoes peeled

1/4 pound lean bacon

1-cup small macaroni

2-jalipeño peppers

2-small onions, or 1-big one

1/2-cup (maybe a little more) milk

1/2 stick (4 TBSP.) butter

(Now for the good stuff that really makes em GREAT)

1/2-TBSP Sunny Caribbee **HERB PEPPER** ☀

1/2-TBSP Sunny Caribbee **SEASONED SEA SALT** ☀

1/2 TBSP Sunny Caribbee unseasoned **SEA SALT**

1/2 or 1/4 TSP Sunny Caribbee **CAYENNE** (depending on just how hot you like things, but, remember, you already have two jalepenos)

Ok, that's everything. Now here's what you do.

Bring a big pot of water and small pot of water to a boil. Throw in 1/4 TBSP unseasoned **SEA SALT** in each pot after it comes to a boil

Cook the potatoes in the big pot and the macaroni in the smaller one.

Chop the bacon in as small pieces as you can.(easy to do when frozen)

Sauté bacon.

Chop the jalipeños small and the onions just a little bigger. Set aside and do not cook.

Drain macaroni, cover well with cold water and set aside.

Drain almost all of the water from the potatoes, put in half the butter and a little milk. Mash 'em.

Add the remainder of the butter and milk and continue to mash.

Now add all the **SUNNY CARIBBEE SPICES** and mix well. Add the jalipeños and onions. Last, gently mix in the macaroni.

Walter Huckabee, Miami, FL

Presto Pesto Pasta

In a small sauce pan combine

1/4 c. **Caribbee's Presto Pesto** ☀

1 – 1-1/2 teas. **Caribbee's Spiced Peppercorns** ☀ (coarsely ground)

1/3 c Pignoli (pine) nuts-unsalted

8-10 lg. mushrooms-cleaned & sliced

3 scallions-diced

3 med. cloves garlic-crushed

3/4 c. extra light olive oil

Simmer on low heat. 30 min. Do <u>not</u> boil & stir frequently

Meanwhile:

Steam until tender but crunchy

2 c broccoli flowerette

2 c cauliflower flowerette

3 med carrots julienned

Cook 12 oz of tri-colored pasta, (or your favorite pasta) Al Dente

Drain pasta but do <u>not</u> rinse.

In a large mixing bowl combine:

hot pasta and steamed vegetables

Toss pasta/vegetables while pouring **Presto Pesto Sauce**. Mixing well
serve with fresh grated Romano/Parmesan cheese

Serves 4-6

Debbie Hatch, Londonderry, NH

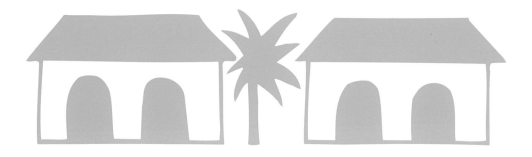

189

Notes

Paradise Pantry

Paradise Pantry is your guided tour to our culinary collection, which originates in Roadtown, Tortola. The tour will conjure up images, aromas and tastes that will tempt you to stock your own pantry with flavour and flair. The tantalizing and bountiful assortment will whet your appetite for creative cooking and enhance the pleasures of tasteful dining.

Familiarizing yourself with the **Paradise Pantry** will enable you to substitute, experiment and increase your knowledge of what goes with what. In case of "Culinary Crisis" ("HELP, I'm out of **Herb Pepper** ☀ !") you can calmly and successfully improvise by consulting your ingredients lists, and creating your own concoction.

Use the "Pantry" as your guide,
Put spice in your life!

B-2 Sauce

(Better than A-1)

An exotic, spicy sauce made with tropical fruit and mildly hot peppers. Enhances the flavours of grilled, stir fried, or baked meat and fish. It adds "zip" to marinades, dips, soups and stews.

Ingredients: vinegar, fruit, water and spices.

BBQ Seasoning

A mildly hot and spicy Caribbean blend with a dash of hickory, adds great character to all your grilled, broiled or pan fried meat recipes, barbecue sauces and marinades.

Ingredients: onion, garlic, celery, salt, chili, hickory and various Caribbean spices.

Bloody Mary Magic

The "Bloody Mary," an enduring classic first served at Harry's Bar in Paris in 1920, is still a brunch-lunch favourite.

Abracadabra! Our "Magic" Mix now easily makes this drink foolproof and perfect every time.

Ingredients: paprika, salt, lemon peel, and other spices.

Caribbee Bouquet Garni

A classic blend with Caribbean spirit is a complete seasoning for the novice or gourmet cook. Flavour soups, stews, casseroles or sauces by adding 1 or 2 hand-made "Bouquets" while cooking.

Ingredients: bay leaf, thyme, rosemary, parsley and other spices.

Caribbean Confections

Jams, Jellies, Chutneys: all made in local kitchens using the finest, freshest fruits, vegetables and Island "Savoir Faire". All have a different season but those usually available are: Papaya Chutney, Mango Chutney, Lime Marmalade, Lime Jelly, Guava Jelly, Hot Pepper Jelly, Papaya Jam, Nutmeg Jam.

West Indian Honey has a unique flavour derived from the fragrant Caribbean flowers and trees.

Caribbee Curry

East meets West

Curry, an ancient and exotic East Indian blend of many spices, combines with aromatic West Indian flavours to create CARIBBEE CURRY.

This innovative, multipurpose seasoning adds zest to a multitude of meat, poultry, fish, egg, cheese and vegetable recipes.

Ingredients: chicken bouillon, curry powder, lemon peel, onion, sesame seed and spices.

Caribbee Hot Sauce

Hot-Hot-Hot

Traditional recipes using flavourful, fiery, pungent peppers and secret spices add "zing to every ting". Used for generations in all the Caribbean countries. "Now...their sauce is your sauce!!"

Handle with care

Caribbee Spiced Tea

A refreshing taste of the Islands: A dry blend of tea, citrus flavours and spices makes a splendid drink, hot or cold, or a flavourful tropical punch.

Down Island Dill

Dill-icious blend of dill, garlic, onion and various seeds and weeds is our newest Total Seasoning. DOWN ISLAND DILL will bring new vitality to old recipes – Escape from the doldrums to the Dill-lightful.

Ingredients: Dill, garlic, onion, sesame and other seeds.

Ginger Beer Syrup

A traditional and tasty Caribbean drink made from the root of the ginger plant and other spices. Also used in glazes, marinades and sauces.

Ingredients: Ginger, sugar, corn starch and other spices.

Ginger Gems

"A delectable sweet with a bit of heat...for sea sickness too, a helpful treat." Crystallized GINGER GEMS are a zesty addition to many recipes, as well as being a piquant digestive after meals.

Guavaberry Liqueur

Rare, indigenous Guavaberries aged in spiced Rum, create this traditional Island Christmas drink. Enjoyable year round, it is also a tasty addition to fruit and dessert recipes.

Herb Pepper Blend

Our HERB PEPPER BLEND has been created to enhance the flavour of most everything...from "soup to nuts". It is especially successful in salad, vegetable and broiled meat recipes. Traditional "Steak au poivre" becomes a new taste sensation!!!

Ingredients: coarse ground pepper, onion, garlic, sea salt, and various herbs.

Island Fish Spice
"Delicious On Fishes"

Slightly hot with a hint of saffron, our tangy blend is very successful when sprinkled on fish to be broiled, baked or grilled. It is excellent in fish soups and stews, such as Bouillabaisse and Cioppino...adds pizazz to fish salads (tuna, crab, shrimp, lobster etc.)

Ingredients: onion, garlic, lemon, saffron, cayenne and other piquant herbs and spices.

Island Nutmeg Mustard

Add water to our unique, secret dry mix to create your own hot, sweet, and spicy mustard. Wonderful on all cold meats, hot dogs, hamburgs and roasts.

Ingredients: hot mustard, brown sugar, salt and spices.

Jerk Sauce

Uniquely Jamaican – used as a marinade on fish, meat or poultry to be grilled, fried, roasted or stewed.

Ingredients: Hot peppers, fruit, vegetables, thyme and spices.

Jerk Seasoning (green)
Uniquely Jamaican

"Jerking" is an authentic Jamaican way to cook. Originating in Boston Beach, a quaint corner of Jamaica, its popularity has quickly and widely spread. JERK SEASONING, is a fiery blend of hot peppers, onions and a special mix of spices and herbs including indigenous and essential pimento (allspice). Use to grill, roast, fry or stew meats, poultry and fish.

Ingredients: onions, garlic, vinegar and assorted herbs.

Jerk Spice (dry)

Hot and full of flavour, dry JERK SPICE can season almost anything that needs a Jamaican Jolt. Use it on marinated meat, fish, poultry before or after cooking and lightly sprinkle on vegetable and cheese dishes.

Ingredients: Allspice, onion, garlic, paprika and other spices.

Kuchela

Authentic Caribbean secret ingredient combining green mangoes, hot red peppers and exotic west Indian spices: KUCHELA is the ideal enhancement to curries, and is used as a marinade and/or a condiment for traditional island cuisine.

Ingredients: mango, mustard oil, amchar massala and spices.

Mauby

MAUBY syrup, made from the bark of a tropical tree and local herbs, is used to make a traditional and refreshing drink. It is particularly popular at carnival time and other festive occasions.

Ingredients: Mauby bark, sugar, corn starch and other spices.

Mild Savory Herbs

MILD SAVORY HERBS is a delicate salt-free medley of 7 herbs: A subtle flavouring for light sauces and soups, egg, tomato and cheese dishes; it enhances fish, chicken, veal and shell-fish recipes. Add toward end of cooking time.

Ingredients: tarragon, chervil, dill, parsley, chives, lemon thyme, savory.

Mixed Hearty Herbs

Our salt-free Caribbean version of the classical Provencal blend, enriches soups, stews, meats and salads. It adds heartiness and character to robust tomato and cheese recipes, herbal butters and dips.

But...be creative!! Cooking is personal art, so experiment and enjoy.

Ingredients: basil, sage, thyme, rosemary, marjoram and other spice.

Plantation Sugar

For your sweet enjoyment.

Amber jewels made from Caribbean cane in the old plantation style, impart liqueur-like flavour and texture to coffee and tea.

A visual and tasteful treat!

Presto Pesto

"A classic"

A contemporary blend of the traditional Italian favourite. Flavourful and fragrant, its many uses are limited only to the imagination. Pizza, pasta, salads, soups, stews and veggies all deserve "Pesto Power".

Ingredients: cheese, garlic, basil, parsley and other herbs.

Seasoned Sea Salt

Sunny Caribbee SEASONED SEA SALT is a traditional West Indian combination of natural sea salt and local flavors which imparts Caribbean "ZIP" to your cuisine.

Ingredients: natural salt, garlic, onion, thyme, parsley and other spices.

Sorrel Syrup

SORREL, a ruby red flower, comes from a plant that is a member of the Hibiscus family. Mixed with West Indian spices, it makes a distinctly different, colourful and refreshing drink. Once a Christmas holiday tradition, Sorrel drinks are now popular the year round. (Mixes well with rum and vodka.)

Ingredients: Sorrel flowers, sugar, cornstarch and other spices.

Spice Island Cocoa Balls

A rare and rich product of the Spice Islands is handmade of pure, natural Cocoa Beans, ground together with a variety of exotic spices. No artificial flavours or preservatives added.

Cocoa balls make a delicious drink and add full, rich flavour to your favourite chocolate recipes.

Spiced Peppercorns

A zesty innovation of red, green, black and white peppercorns with fragrant allspice. Our colourful and flavourful mix has a special taste and aroma.

Spicee Catsup

A sugar-free and delicious West Indian innovation created with all natural ingredients and enhanced by island spices

So rich and thick...it should be "spooned".

So unique and flavourful you can't do without !!

Ingredients: vinegar, tomato puree and other spices.

Steak Spice

A hot and crunchy no-salt alternative to traditional BBQ seasonings. It perks up ordinary broiled, grilled or sauteed meat recipes, as well as adding a new dimension to potato salad and bland veggies.

(shake before using)

Ingredients: caraway seed, coriander, mustard seed, garlic and other natural seasonings.

Sugar 'N' Spice
(and everything nice)

SUGAR 'N' SPICE is our versatile blend of natural brown sugar and tropical spices..an interesting topping for pancakes, puddings and hot or cold cereal. A small amount will impart a wonderful spiciness to hot tea or coffee or rum punch.

Sprinkle in or add to cookie and cake batters before baking. Use in glazed vegetable and fruit recipes to create excitement.

Ingredients: brown sugar and spices.

Sunshine Salsa

Put sunshine and fire in your cuisine with hot and spicy SUNSHINE SALSA mix.
A Caribbean blend of "South Of The Border" flavours makes a sizzling salsa and a spirited addition to many recipes. Olé Olé.

Ingredients: peppers, onion, tomatoes and other spices.

197

Super Spice

Our zesty mixture of herbs, garlic, cheese, sesame and poppy seeds is the "for everyting" seasoning: Vegetables, salads, chicken, pasta, garlic bread. Let your imagination be your guide!!

(shake before using)

Tangy Tropical Ting
Authentic Creole Creation

An expertly balanced blend of mild heat and full spicy Tropical flavour which imparts the exotic taste of the Islands...A sensational dipping or basting sauce, marinade or perfect condiment to enhance all meals.

Ingredients: Garlic, chives, onion, soy sauce and spices.

Vanilla-Vanilla
Double the Flavour

Pure vanilla extract is 100% natural, having a delicate but distinctive taste and bouquet not found in imitations.

"A bean in every bottle" releases concentrated aromatic richness.

West Indian Green

Our amazing, versatile, and flavourful sauce with a unique, fresh taste. For marinades, salad dressings, dips, spreads and the "as is" Caribbean condiment extraordinaire for meat, fish, cheese and eggs.

"Makes every meal a masterpiece!"

Ingredients: green herbs, salt, pepper, garlic, onion.

West Indian Rum Peppers

Made with finest local rum, fresh peppers and spices...WEST INDIAN RUM PEPPERS adds pizazz to hundreds of dishes: stews, soups, marinades, curries, egg and cheese recipes, and "Bloody Marys". It's hot!!

West Indian Vinegar

Distinctive Caribbean style vinegars made with local herbs, spices, fruits and vegetables. A unique addition to salads, marinades and sauces, our vinegars also intensify blending of flavours when sprinkled on fish, meat, veggies and into soups and stews.

Herbs, Spices, Seeds and Seasonings

Spices are obtained from bark, roots or berries of perennial plants (Ginger, Nutmeg, Cloves, Cinnamon, Allspice, Pepper, etc.)

Herbs are leaves of annual and perennial plants (Basil, Tarragon, Parsley, Dill, Rosemary, etc.)

Aromatic Seeds come from flowering, lacy annual plants (Celery, Dill Fennel, Poppy, Caraway, Sesame, etc.)

Seasonings or Blends are mixtures of many spices and/or herbs. (Chili Powder, Curry Powder) or Specialty Blends like all of our Sunny Caribbee mixed seasonings: **Herb Pepper** ☀, **Seasoned Sea Salt** ☀, **Super Spice** ☀, etc.

Herbal Hints

1. The strength of herbs and spices can vary with brand, age and condition. Often "to taste" is exactly that. Recipe measurements are only a guide.
2. Herbs, spices, and seasonings should be kept in a cool, dry, dark place – to retain flavour and colour. Whole spices keep longer than ground ones and herbs have a relatively short shelf life. Don't ruin your food with "worn-out" faded and flavourless herbs and spices.
3. Add **ground** spices or herbs towards end of cooking time. **Whole** spices (**Bouquet Garni** for ex.) are added at beginning of cooking time. For uncooked recipes, herbs and spices should be allowed to mellow with other ingredients for a long time.
4. 1 tsp. dried herbs or seasonings equals approximately 1 Tbs. fresh.
5. Use an herb grinder or crush herbs between your fingers to release maximum aroma and flavour.

Sunny Caribbee Spice List

Allspice, ground
Allspice, whole
Anise Seed
Anise, Star
Annatto
Arrowroot
Basil
Bayleaf
Caraway Seed
Cardamon
Celery Salt
Celery Seed
Chervil
Chili Peppers
Chili Powder (blend)
Chinese 5 Spice
   (blend)
Cilantro
Cinnamon, ground
Cinnamon Sticks
Cloves, ground
Cloves, whole
Coriander, ground
Coriander, whole
Cumin, ground
Cumin, whole
Curry, Madras
Curry Powder, hot
   (blend)
Curry Powder, mild
   (blend)
Dill Seed
Dill Weed
Fennel Seed
Fenugreek, whole
Garam Masala

(blend)
Garlic Chips
Ginger, ground
Ginger, whole
Lemon Peel
   (granules)
Mace, whole
Marjoram, cut
Mustard, ground
Mustard Seed
Nutmeg, ground
Nutmeg, whole
Onion Chips
Oregano
Paprika
Parsley Flakes
Pepper, black,
   ground
Pepper, Cayenne
Peppercorns,
   black, whole
Peppercorns,
   green
Peppercorns, pink
Peppercorns, white
Poppy Seed
Rosemary
Saffron
Sage, Rubbed
Summer Savory
Sea Salt Crystals
Sesame Seed
Tarragon
Thyme
Turmeric, ground
Vanilla Beans

Tropical Teas

At **Sunny Caribbee**, we have an excellent selection of Teas, both Flavoured and Herbal. These Teas are an all natural, low calorie, convenient and economical way to quench your thirst.

The Flavoured Teas are composed of fine black tea combined with Island Spices, local dried fruit or other tropical flavours, all making delightful hot or cold drinks:

Cinnamon Spiced
Ginger
Lemon Spiced
Mango
Orange Spiced
Passionfruit
Rum

Caffeine-free Herbal Teas are legendary in the West Indies. Many are served solely for flavour, but traditionally, **Herbal Teas**, are recognized for their restorative, relaxing and medicinal powers. **"Bush" Teas** have been an important part of Caribbean culture for centuries, originating with slaves from Africa and the indigenous Carib and Arawak Indians.

Breadfruit—treats high blood pressure
Chamomile—stimulates appetite and soothes nerves
Eucalyptus— soothes sore throats and symptoms of bronchitis
Herbal Blend—is a complete Multi-Purpose tonic
Hibiscus—increases energy and comforts stomach disorders
Papaya—brings relief from pain due to heartburn and gas.
Passionflower—eases nervous tension, headaches, hysteria and pain from arthritis
Sour Sop—treats colds, fever and insomnia
Sunny Caribbee Specialty Herbal Blends: West Indian Hangover Cure and **Arawak Love Potion** — self explanatory treatment.

Herbal teas need a longer steeping time than black tea. Use approximately 1 tsp. dried leaves for each tea cup of water and let steep in non-metallic pot. Add lemon and honey for more flavour.

Coffees from the Caribbean

Coffee is grown in a number of Caribbean countries, mainly those having fertile, cool, mountainous areas. Jamaica, Haiti, Dominican Republic, Puerto Rico, Cuba and Trinidad are amongst the best known Coffee producing countries of the world, whose mountains have the requisite cool temperatures, extra shade and moderate rainfall.

The Coffee Trees are 10-15 feet high at maturity yielding clusters of "beans" that turn red when ripe. The Caribbean Beans are usually dark roasted to maximize the rich full bodied flavour.

At **Sunny Caribbee** we have two specialty Coffees: **Tropical Blend** ☀, a combination of several Caribbean Coffees and **Spice Coffee** ☀ which is ground with tropical spices. Other Coffees that are usually available:

Jamaican High Mountain
Puerto Rican
Haitian
Trinidad
Santa Domingo

Dash, Splash and Sprinkle

Dash, Splash and Sprinkle is my style of cooking. You might call it "no recipe cooking." For those of you who also get bored following long recipes or just like to have some fun experimenting in the kitchen, this section has two purposes:

1. to aquaint you with additional uses for our sauces, seasonings and condiments. **Steak Spice** ☀ doesn't always have to be used for steak or **Fish Spice** ☀ for fish...

2. to liberate you from conventional cooking methods by encouraging you to experiment and to create your own personal cuisine.

We don't always have to follow recipes to the letter, measure every ingredient, or accept the limitations of someone else's taste. We should trust our own imagination and instincts and enjoy the adventure of our own creations.

(Write your own successful ideas and discoveries in the blank spaces)

B-2 Sauce

1. Splash into gravies or stews.
2. Splash onto meatloaf or hamburgers before cooking.
3. Dash into meat marinades.
4. Spread on bread or buns for sandwiches.

_____

_____

_____

_____

BBQ Seasoning

1. Sprinkle on meat before grilling, frying, roasting.
2. Add to **Spicee Catsup** ☀ for BBQ sauce (also add hot sauce).
3. Add to baked beans.
4. Sprinkle into chili, taco mixture.
5. Sprinkle on popcorn.
6. Add a dash to guacamole.
7. Sprinkle on onions or potatoes and other vegetables before roasting or grilling.
8. Add several dashes to flour for chicken or fish coating.
9. Enhance flavours of most Mexican or South Western recipes.

10. Use instead of salt in marinades and salad dressing.

_____

_____

_____

_____

Bloody Mary Magic

1. Sprinkle into potato salad, chicken, egg or tuna salad.
2. Sprinkle into or mix with tomato or V-8 juice.
3. Dash some into tomato or other vegetable soup.
4. Add to seafood dressing.

_____

_____

_____

_____

Caribbee Bouquet Garni

1. Add to poaching water for chicken or fish.
2. Add to liquid when making stews or soups

3. Simmer with packaged or canned soups for more flavour.

_____

_____

_____

_____

CARIBBEAN CONFECTIONS
West Indian Honey

1. Replaces sugar in many recipes
2. Splash onto waffles and pancakes instead of syrup.
3. Glaze meat or veggies.
4. Make honey butter for toast, muffins, fruit or nut breads, pancakes. Whip together 1 c. unsalted butter or margarine, 1/3 c. honey and tsp. grated orange peel.
5. Sweeten tea, coffee or punch.

_____

_____

_____

_____

Jams and Jellies

1. Spread between cake or cookie layers.
2. Glaze meat to be roasted or broiled.
3. Put 2 tbs. muffin or cupcake batter in bottom of greased muffin tin. Add 1 1/2 tsp. preserve, fill tin 3/4 full and bake as usual.
4. Fill tarts or "turnovers".
5. Thin with juice and pour over ice cream.

_____

_____

_____

_____

_____

Chutney

1. Combine with sour cream for quick dip.
2. Use as glaze for poultry or ham.
3. Serve with Cheese and Crackers.
4. Sandwich spread for cold meats.
5. Dash a bit into chicken, pork, beef or egg salad.
6. Add a dash to muffin batter.

7. Perfect condiment to make any meal special.

_____

_____

_____

_____

_____

_____

Caribbee Curry

1. Mix with mayonnaise for meat sauce, salad dressing or dip.
2. Mix with butter for vegetables.
3. Add to devilled eggs or quiche.
4. Dash a bit into chicken pie stock or chicken gravy.
5. Dash into potato salad or scalloped potatoes.
6. Add to puff pastry or biscuit mix.
7. Add to cream sauces or soups.
8. Add to gravy to make instant curried lamb, beef or pork.

_____

_____

_____

_____

_____

_____

Caribbee Nutmeg Kit

Sprinkle freshly ground nutmeg on:
- Rum punch
- Fruit cup
- Puddings
- Cookies
- Milk shakes and egg nog
- Granola with yogurt
- Fruit and yogurt
- Dessert coffees

_____

_____

_____

_____

_____

_____

Caribbee Hot Sauce

1. Splash into:
- Barbecue sauce.
- Chili and other bean dishes.
- Tacos, burritos, fajitas, enchiladas and all Mexican, South Western or Caribbean recipes.
- Dips and soups.

2.Dash onto:
- Hot dogs, Hamburger's, and cold meat sandwiches.
- Egg and cheese dishes.

_____

_____

_____

_____

_____

Down Island Dill

1. Sprinkle on:
   - Sliced tomatoes and cucumber
   - Broiled tomatoes.
2. Add to:
   - Potato salad
   - Chicken salad
   - Fish salads
   - Egg salad
3. Dash into:
   - White sauce
   - Scalloped or mashed potato
   - Noodle or other pasta dishes
   - Cold vegetable soups or dips, cottage or cream cheese for cocktail spreads
   - Mayonnaise and/or sour cream, for a fish sauce

5. Make dill butter:
   1 tsp. dill to 1/4 lb. butter for:
   - Popcorn.
   - Toasted grilled French or other bread.
   - To dress vegetables or fish.

_____

_____

_____

_____

_____

Ginger Beer Syrup

1. Splash over fruit, cake or ice cream.
2. Sprinkle into your meat marinades
3. Glaze meats before roasting.
4. Glaze vegetables.
5. Splash a bit into hot or iced tea.
6. Add a dash to rum punch or mulled cider.

_____

_____

_____

_____

_____

Ginger Gems

1. Add chopped pieces to ice cream or sherbet.
2. Add to fruit cup.
3. Mix chopped gems into cookie, cake or muffin mix (bran muffins particularly good !)
4. Add to rice or bread pudding.

_____

_____

_____

_____

_____

Herb Pepper Blend

Sprinkle on:

- Salads
- Veggies
- All meats and fish
- Popcorn
- Rice
- Pasta
- Dips
- Soups
- Sauces
- Everything that needs special flavour

_____

_____

_____

_____

_____

_____

Island Fish Spice

Sprinkle:

- into fish salads: tuna, salmon, shrimp, lobster.
- on fish to be grilled, baked or fried.
- into sauces for fish.
- into fish soups or stews, Cioppino, Bouillabaisse, Jambalaya, Gumbo.
- into poaching water for fish.

_____

_____

_____

_____

_____

Island Nutmeg Mustard

1. Mix with sour cream for dip.
2. Mix with honey to make meat glaze.
3. Brush prepared mustard and oil on poultry, fish, meat to be barbecued.

4. Add to salad dressing.

5. Dash a bit into bean casseroles.

6. Add to cooked white sauce to make a mustard sauce.

_____

_____

_____

_____

_____

_____

Jerk Sauce

1. Glaze meats before roasting.

2. Mix with oil for marinade.

3. Splash into sauces or gravies.

4. Splash into soup or stew needing "pizzazz."

5. Lightly spread on bread before making sandwiches.

6. Splash into cheese, meat or vegetable casseroles.

_____

_____

_____

_____

_____

Jerk Seasoning (green)

1. Marinate meat or fish with Seasoning, to be baked.

2. Add several good splashes to poaching water.

3. Mix with oil for a marinade to be used on broiled food.

4. Mix with mayonnaise for a spice sauce or condiment.

6. Thin with milk for salad dressing.

7. Use as a "relish" on hamburgers or other hot or cold sandwiches.

_____

_____

_____

_____

_____

Jerk Spice (dry)

1. Add to rice.

2. Dash into stews or casseroles.

3. Sprinkle on or in ground meat before cooking.

4. Sprinkle on poultry, meat or fish to be grilled.

5. Add to marinades.

_____

_____

_____

_____

Kuchela

1. Use the same way as you would use **Jerk Seasoning** ☀ but realize the **Kuchela** has more "heat".
2. Use as a condiment to meat or fish dishes especially curries.

_____

_____

_____

_____

_____

Mauby ("Caribbean Bitters")

1. Dash **Mauby** any place that you would use "bitters":
   • Drinks • Sauces • Soup
   • Gravy • Jellies • Fruit Pies
   • Cooked or preserved fruit
   • Dash into a glass of water for a digestive drink

_____

_____

_____

_____

_____

Mild Savory Herbs

1. Sprinkle on or in:
   • Scrambled eggs.
   • Fish, egg, chicken salad
   • Boiled eggs
   • Creamed sauces or soups
   • Cheese dishes
   • Rice
   • Tomatoes
   • Marinades
2. Mix with bread crumbs to coat fish or poultry
3. Mix with mayo for fish or chicken accompaniment.
4. Mix with butter to dress vegetables.
5. Add with salt and pepper to oil and vinegar for salad dressing.
6. Dash into fish or chicken poaching water.

_____

_____

_____

_____

_____

Mixed Hearty Herbs

1. Sprinkle on or in:
   - Pizza and pasta
   - Salads
   - Potatoes
   - Veggies
   - Stews and Soup
   - Omelets and egg dishes
   - Rice
2. Mix with cream cheese, yogurt or sour cream for dip or sauce.
3. Mix with butter for vegetables or bread.
4. Make seasoned bread crumbs.
5. Mix with butter or oil for quick pasta sauce.
6. Add to vinaigrette salad dressing.

_____
_____
_____
_____
_____

Plantation Sugar

1. A festive replacement for ordinary sugar in hot tea or coffee.
2. Add to a cake or muffin batter.
3. Sprinkle a few crystals on cookie batter before baking.
4. Sprinkle on cake frosting for tasty and decorative effect.

_____
_____
_____
_____
_____
_____

Presto Pesto

1. Sprinkle on or in:
   - Popcorn
   - Salads
   - Pasta or pasta sauces
   - Soups
   - Scrambled eggs or omelettes
   - Uncooked biscuits or rolls before baking
   - Sliced tomatoes and cucumbers
   - Mashed or baked potatoes

2.Make **Pesto Butter:**

2–3 tsp. **Presto Pesto** ☀ to 1/2 c. butter

- To dress veggies, steak or fish
- For clam or mussel dipping
- Instant sauce for pasta or rice
- Sauté with vegetables or fish
- Spread for "Garlic bread" or toast or croutons

3. **Pesto Mayonnaise:**

1-1/2 – 2 Tbs. **Presto Pesto** ☀ to 1 c. mayonnaise

- Mix with chicken cubes or shell fish
- Mix with cubed potatoes or other veggies
- Add sour cream and use as dip

_____
_____
_____
_____
_____

Seasoned Sea Salt

Natural sea salt, plus the addition of fresh island seasoning, enhances all foods where flavour needs a boost. Because of the additional seasoning, less salt is necessary. A healthy and tasty consideration.

Sprinkle on:
- Veggies
- Meat and Fish
- Soups and sauces
- Salads
- Pasta
- Rice
- Any where that salt would usually be needed

_____
_____
_____
_____
_____
_____

Sorrel Syrup

1. Splash into fruit dishes
2. Add to fruit glazes.
3. Splash into iced tea or other cold drinks.
4. Replacement for cranberry juice in drink and dessert recipes.

_____
_____
_____
_____
_____

Spice Island Cocoa Balls

1. Grate on ice cream or pudding.
2. Sprinkle grated **Cocoa Balls** ☀ into cake or cookie batter.
3. Sprinkle grated **Cocoa Balls** ☀ over dessert coffees.
4. Use in any recipe where chocolate is needed.

_____
_____
_____
_____

Spiced Peppercorns (mixed)

1. Grind on or into:
   - Veggies
   - Meat and poultry
   - Fish
   - Egg dishes
   - Soups and sauces
   - Stews
   - Salads
   - Any where that you would use pepper, but enjoy the extra flavour and zing of **Spiced Peppercorns** ☀.

2. Hors D'oeuvre:

   Pepper Spiced Chèvre

   1/2 lb. montrachet or other chèvre (goat cheese rounds)
   - Grind **Spiced Peppercorns** ☀ until you have 3-tsp.
   - Cut cheese into 2 rounds and roll in ground pepper, coating well.
   - Serve at room temp.

_____
_____
_____
_____

Spicee Catsup

1. Mix with **Hot Sauce** ☀ and **BBQ Seasoning** ☀ to make instant barbecue sauce or marinade.
2. Mix with mayonnaise to make salad dressing.
3. Splash into bean salads.
5. Dash a bit into taco, burrito, sloppy joe recipes.
6. A wonderful condiment for cold or hot meat and fish dishes.
7. Add horse radish and **Hot Sauce** ☀ for fish dipping sauce.

8. Brush on meat loaf before baking.

_____
_____
_____
_____
_____
_____

Steak Spice

1. Mix with hamburger or other ground meat before cooking.
2. Add to potato or tuna salad.
3. Dash some into meatloaf mix.
4. Add to marinades.
5. Splash a good bit into poaching water.
6. Sprinkle on any meat to be grilled, broiled or roasted.
7. Sprinkle on bland veggies.

_____
_____
_____
_____
_____

Sugar 'N' Spice

1. Sprinkle on fresh fruit.
2. Sprinkle on cereal (hot or old).
3. Sprinkle on baked butternut, acorn or other winter squash or pumpkin.
4. Sprinkle on top of cup cakes or muffins before baking.
5. Use in place of white sugar in coffee, tea, cocoa or punch.
6. Sprinkle on baked fruit dishes.
7. Add to puddings and custards.
8. Make "Caribbee Toast": Butter toast, then freely sprinkle with **Sugar 'N' Spice** ☀. Place under broiler 'til brown and bubbly.

_____
_____
_____
_____
_____

Sunshine Salsa

1. Prepared **Salsa** (p. 76):
   • Filling for "Spanish Omelettes".
   • Topping for fried or poached eggs.
   • Accompaniment for hash, barbecue and roasted meats.
   • Topping for baked potatoes

- Condiment for hot dogs, hamburgers and tacos.
- Dash a bit on sandwiches.
- Add to corn, bean or rice salads
- Splash into guacamole.

2. Dry salsa mix:
   - Use in meatloaf or hamburg recipes.
   - Add to chili, enchilada, burrito recipes.
   - Mix with mayonnaise, cream cheese or yogurt for tortilla dip.
   - Dissolve in tomato juice and add to rice—"Instant Mexican Rice"

_____
_____
_____
_____
_____
_____

Super Spice

1. Sprinkle on:
   - Cooked buttered vegetables
   - Popcorn
   - Salads
   - Pasta or rice
   - Baked potatoes

2. Dash or splash a bit into quiche or omelettes.
3. Mix with sour cream, cottage cheese or yogurt for veggie dip.
4. Sprinkle on buttered breadsticks, brown under broiler.

_____
_____
_____
_____
_____
_____

Tangy Tropical Ting

1. Glaze meats before roasting.
2. Mix with oil for meat marinade.
3. Splash into stews, meat or bean casseroles.
4. Splash into brown sauce or gravy.
5. Spread on bread for sandwiches.
6. Condiment for any meal.
7. Use as a dipping sauce for fondue, satays or other skewered meats.

_____
_____
_____
_____
_____
_____

Vanilla-Vanilla

1. Splash into Coca Cola for "Back to the Fifties" treat.

2. Splash a dash into mixed fruit, cold or baked.

3. Splash into all your baking recipes.

4. Dash a bit and mix with your coffee beans before grinding.

5. Splash into milk shakes, eggnog and other milk or ice cream drinks.

_____

_____

_____

_____

_____

West Indian Green

1. Spread on bread for sandwiches especially fish, chicken or egg.

2. Mix with mayonnaise for shrimp or scallop dip.

3. Add to marinades and salad dressing.

4. Table condiment for meat, fish, cheese and egg dishes.

5. An excellent fondue sauce.

_____

_____

_____

_____

West Indian Rum Peppers

1. Splash into:
   - Bloody Marys
   - Beef stew
   - Chili
   - Cheese sauce or fondue
   - Marinades
   - Curries
   - Egg dishes
   - Fish soups

_____

_____

_____

_____

West Indian Vinegar

1. Splash into salads with oil, or combine with seasonings for salad dressing.
2. Use in marinades.
3. Sprinkle on fish, meat, veggies to intensify flavour.
4. Use in sauces.
5. For wine substitute in many recipes.

_____

_____

_____

_____

Notes

Product Index

Sunny Caribbee Specialty　　　Helpful Hints　　　Can be made ahead

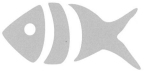

Recipe Index

☀ Sunny Caribbee Specialty   ≋ Helpful Hints   ☾ Can be made ahead

227

☀ ORDER MORE SUNSHINE STYLE ☀

ORDERED BY:
ORDER BY:
MAIL, FAX OR PHONE

Name:

Street or Box No.

City

State   Zip

DAYTIME PHONE ☐☐☐☐ - ☐☐☐ - ☐☐☐☐

SHIP TO:
Fill in ONLY if different from "ORDERED BY:"

Name:

Street or Box No.

City

State   Zip

ORDERS TO ADDITIONAL ADDRESSES:
1. Use a blank piece of paper to make out a separate order for each address.
2. Be sure to indicaate both your own and recipient's name and address.
3. Each address requires separate postage.

Is this a Gift? ☐ yes ☐ no   **Ship When?** ☐ At once ☐ To arrive on

___ COPIES	☀ SUNSHINE STYLE	@ $ 22.50	$
		postage and handling @ $2.50	
		TOTAL ENCLOSED	$

Payment Method: Make checks payable to **SUNNY CARIBBEE SPICE CO.**

☐ Check or Money order

☐ Master Card/ Visa

☐ American Express

Credit Card Account Number

☐☐☐☐ - ☐☐☐☐ - ☐☐☐☐ - ☐☐☐☐   EXP.DATE

MO./YR.

AUTHORIZED SIGNATURE_____

Orders outside the U.S. must include Credit Card Number for exact Shipping charges.

MAIL, FAX ,OR PHONE TO:
SUNNY CARIBBEE SPICE COMPANY MAIL ORDER SERVICE -
Telephone: 809-494-2178   Fax: 809-494-4039

P.O. BOX 3237 VDA
ST. THOMAS, USVI
00803-3237

- - - - - - - - - - - - - - - - - cut on dotted line - - - - - - - - - - - - - - - - -

To stock your **PARADISE PANTRY**, order FREE Full-Color catalog below:

ORDERED BY:
ORDER BY:
MAIL, FAX OR PHONE

Name:

Street or Box No.

City

State   Zip

DAYTIME PHONE ☐☐☐☐ - ☐☐☐ - ☐☐☐☐

SHIP TO:
Fill in ONLY if different from "ORDERED BY:"

Name:

Street or Box No.

City

State   Zip

MAIL, FAX ,OR PHONE TO:
SUNNY CARIBBEE SPICE COMPANY MAIL ORDER SERVICE -
Telephone: 809-494-2178   Fax: 809-494-4039

P.O. BOX 3237 VDA
ST. THOMAS, USVI
00803-3237